Evolving Regional Economies

Evolving Regional Economies

Resources, Specialization, Globalization

Martin Henning

agenda
publishing

First published in 2022 by Agenda Publishing

Agenda Publishing Limited
The Core
Bath Lane
Newcastle Helix
Newcastle upon Tyne
NE4 5TF
www.agendapub.com

ISBN 978-1-78821-407-0 (hardcover)
ISBN 978-1-78821-408-7 (paperback)

British Library Cataloguing-in-Publication Data
A catalogue record for this book is available from the British Library

Typeset by Newgen Publishing UK
Printed and bound in the UK by CPI Group (UK) Ltd, Croydon, CR0 4YY

Contents

Acknowledgements

The ideas in this book are of course not all my own. Some are, but many are owed, as are most incremental innovations, to combinations of ideas that other scholars came up with. In particular, my way of thinking about regional economic change has developed during my joint work with Frank Neffke, Karl-Johan Lundquist and Lars-Olof Olander. Ron Boschma generously introduced me to the idea of evolutionary economic geography. Two Claeses – Claes-Göran Alvstam and Claes Svensson – have been generous enough to read the manuscript in detail and provide many suggestions for improvements. I am also grateful for constructive comments from an anonymous reviewer. Alison Howson at Agenda Publishing has provided many excellent editorial suggestions. This book is based on research generously funded by Länsförsäkringar Alliance Research Foundation.

Martin Henning

1

Regional economies, but global too

> The division between a distinct time perspective and a distinct spatial perspective is something given by tradition, and something which I perceive as a weakness.
>
> T. Hägerstrand, "Tidsgeografi", 134 (author's translation)

The importance of regional economic change and long-term growth

Regional economic change and long-term regional growth are important processes, because they directly affect the livelihoods of people. How regions cope with economic change, and what the longer-term growth patterns of regions look like, affect people's income, their living conditions and probably their decisions to stay in a region or to move out of it. To talk about regional economies is to talk about people's welfare. This book explores an evolutionary perspective on the processes of regional economic change and long-term regional growth.

Economic change is a story about how the lives of our recent ancestors gradually improved. Most of us, except a fortunate few, know that only 150 or 200 years ago, our ancestors were poor, living under very sparse material conditions, probably working in or close to the agricultural sector, which demanded hard labour, and with potentially fatal diseases lurking around every corner. At times, our recent ancestors might also have had to emigrate to make a better life for themselves in another country, if conditions and regulations even allowed moving outside their region. In many parts of the world, this is still true.

By an amazing process of economic change and growth, especially following the second industrial revolution in the 1800s, working conditions and living standards have improved greatly, at least in the "industrialized" economies.

This process of change and growth has not been purely economic though. It has been intertwined with extraordinary developments in technologies, as well as changes in institutions and social relationships, creating new opportunities for our recent ancestors and, in that way, for many of our generation also.

Better and more efficient markets for goods and services, and for labour too, have been important drivers of this change. However, markets do not work unless they are partially regulated and monitored. Governments have important roles to play here. Regional and national governments need to make sure that some valuable resources that markets are not that good at catering for, such as well-functioning educational systems, exist.

Even though most things have become much better for most people in the longer run, the promising processes of regional economic change have not been without considerable downsides. When regional economic conditions get better on average, there are also those that lose out in processes of change. These could be people that suffer from inadequate working conditions, are being paid wages that are too low or become displaced from their jobs. By means of social security systems, better labour market regulations and stricter ethical codes of conduct, firms and governments have addressed some of these concerns in some countries and regions, but much remains to be done for large parts of the globe. Historically, industrial development and improved market economies have certainly led to a general uplift in living standards, but it has not been an unequivocal success.

In many parts of the world, people are still struggling hard to provide a minimal living standard for themselves and their families. By learning more about how economic change and long-term regional growth works, we will be able to improve conditions for further economic change so that more people can benefit from economic growth.

Today, processes of regional economic change also have to link to how we address the great environmental challenges of our time. It is true that industrialization has drastically improved material and economic well-being for billions of people across the globe. However, it is equally true that this has come at the expense of our natural environment, stretching its resilience to the limit, or even beyond. Future economic change must incorporate a more efficient use of resources and decrease its ecological footprint. It can be debated whether this is achievable within the framework of our current "marketized" organization of the economy. However, the historical failure to organize alternative regimes so far gives little hope for other ways of tackling the issue than a reformed market economy.

Lots of insightful books and articles already deal with different aspects of economic growth. In this book, we take a closer look at economic growth and change as geographical processes. This geographical view is important, because processes of growth and change differ considerably across regions, and often within the same country. The core aim of this particular book is to show how geography conditions economic change and growth, or rather, how resources, people and firms within a specific geography condition economic change within it. The regional view makes economic change more interesting, because it brings the economic processes close to people and their everyday lives.

Yet, geography is not quite enough to provide a relevant framework for understanding regional economic change. Because we are talking about regional economic change as a process, time needs to come into consideration. In fact, geography and history intertwine inseparably, and history conditions economic change and growth too, or rather, events that take place over time and the legacies they leave behind condition it.

This is not quite the first attempt to synthesize these two core aspects of human life – space and time – in economic analysis. Nevertheless, it has proven incredibly difficult to take both time and space into account within one unified framework when analysing and explaining regional growth and change. Building on recent research achievements, this book develops a theoretical perspective on how to combine both time and space in order to understand regional economic change better.

It is important to note that "conditioned" by history is very different from "determined" by history. This distinction is common among evolutionary scholars and is important. It captures the fact that it is possible to escape the structures of geography and history and the paths of regional economic change that they suggest. However, escaping them often requires no little effort and knowledge to achieve it.

In sum, the perspective throughout this book is "productionist": we are mainly interested in how and where the production of goods and services actually takes place, and how and why it changes over time.

A regional lens on a global economy, where distances matter less and places matter more

In a global economy there are actually plenty of arguments why we should *not* focus on how geography and history condition economic activities. Video conferences link up the globe, and if you need to transport goods or travel, it is comfortable, safe and relatively cheap. From the late 1990s, at least until the Covid-19 pandemic, the general sentiment was that we are living in an increasingly functionally integrated global economy, as communications become cheaper and both trade and cross-border investments increase (Dicken 2015;

Buckley, Enderwick & Cross 2018). Why do we need to consider geography and history in such a globally integrated and fast-changing world?

BOX 1.1 REGIONS

"Region" is a tricky but useful concept and can be defined in many different ways. The economic geographer Gunnar Törnqvist (2000) defined four kinds of regions: natural, cultural, functional and administrative. Common to all of these is that they consider regions as subnational entities (smaller than average countries). Today, economic geographers and regional scientists tend to rely mostly on functional and administrative definitions of regions. Administrative regions are those decided formally by states or authorities on different levels, such as provinces, counties or planning areas. Functional regions are defined by the average linkages between places. These could be commuting patterns, contact structures or market areas for retail. Labour market regions and city regions are currently probably the most used functional varieties. Throughout this book, a "region" will always refer to a functional region.

As one attentive observer has noted, the fact that distance becomes less important does not mean that places – or rather, what goes on in places – becomes less important (*Economist* 2012). There are a couple of reasons why we should hold that to be true. A very superficial look at the matter would lead us to conclude that geography and history make a difference to economic change and growth because:

1. With globalization, geographical distance has become less important but not completely unimportant. Distance still represents a friction or an obstacle that affects many types of economic transactions. Goods need to be transported to reach customers and markets, and people and ideas need to be transported too. So far, there is still a geographical interaction cost associated with this, whether it is a traditional transportation charge or a loss of information. Also, geography is actually not only about physical distance but about the institutions and power relations that influence how different places link to each other too. There are different forms of "proximities" apart from geographical proximity – cognitive, organizational, social and institutional – that relate to geography in different ways and affect the outcomes of economic transactions in space (Boschma 2005).
2. During globalization, economic activities take place in particular localities for a reason, and regions specialize. This means that regions often develop

distinct production profiles or even clusters. It is common that regions become widely associated with their economic specialties. Silicon Valley (IT), Hollywood (film and entertainment), the City of London (financial activities), Ingolstadt (automobiles), Nagoya (air and aviation industries) and Bangalore (IT services) are just some of the well-known regional specializations. Apart from these, there are thousands of less famous regional specializations across all economies. There is a reason for that, or actually several. Places are still important.

3. Some regions have a difficult time escaping their economic past. The Ruhr area in Germany, for example, once the industrial heartland of the European continent, has struggled to remain relevant in a time of deindustrialization and a growing service economy. Much the same goes for old industrial regions in the UK, the USA, Scandinavia and eastern Europe. Places, or rather what they contain, seem to matter not only "now" but for the "future" too.

These examples suggest that we need to consider space and place if we want to understand how the economy unfolds over time and how that affects people. This is true in a globalized economy too. We will call that a regional lens, and we will try to apply it to the analysis of economic growth and change (Bathelt & Glückler 2003).

An important argument in this book is that economic activities and economic change are inevitably linked to a place, but they are linked to other places too. Today's globalized economy builds on sophisticated regional specialization patterns that have developed over some time. Globalization has been a process of functional integration between regions with specialized production profiles (Dicken 2015). This also means that regional economies have become more dependent on each other. Regional specialization and exchange, underpinned by the use of different regional resources in thousands of places, conditions the nearly endless repertoire of products maintained by the global economy today.

BOX 1.2 GLOBALIZATION

Globalization is used to describe how economies across the globe have become more interdependent for several reasons (Dicken 2015):

- Faster information sharing between locations with ICT technologies;
- Cheaper, faster and safer transportation across the globe;
- Increasing trade and trade liberalization;
- Linked financial markets;

- Relocation of some manufacturing from North America and Europe to lower-cost countries;
- Growth of countries in South East Asia as producer and consumption countries, especially China;
- The growth of trans-national corporations; and
- More complex ownership patterns.

On average, the globalization process has coincided with huge improvements in the economic standards of countries. However, it has been noted that to some countries and regions globalization has meant little actual change, and in particular places globalization has even had adverse effects.

A continued increase in global material wealth requires an even more sophisticated pattern of regional specialization. If we were to move towards a less integrated global economy, many of the benefits of regional specialization would also be lost. This would do immense damage to the global economic system and to our welfare too. In fact, regional and national economic protectionism is far worse today than it used to be when regions were more self-sufficient. The more complex the economy becomes, the more interaction across nations and regions we need.

Therefore, understanding the economic geography of a globalized world in a profound way requires a sophisticated regional lens that balances what goes on within regions with what goes on between them.

A regional lens on what firms do

If we consider the economy in finer detail, at the level of the firms themselves, the regional lens is equally important. The successes of firms are intertwined with the resources available in their surrounding regions. In economic geography, traditional location analysis has made this strikingly obvious, although interest in these classical approaches was motivated primarily by cost-minimization considerations and not by a prime interest in economic change.

Very few firms are isolated from their regional environments. Labour is normally sourced locally and appropriate local infrastructure is essential to the operation of most firms. In other words, the regional resources offered to firms, for example by the regional labour market and by the local infrastructure, affect both the operations of firms and their potential to innovate and renew. This is not a new argument. Since the 1990s many scholars in geography and neighbouring disciplines have made this point (Storper 1997; Maskell & Malmberg 1999a; Porter 2003).

Therefore, to understand how firms themselves grow, develop and change, we cannot only look at what is taking place inside firms. A regional lens needs to be applied here too.

For some firms, this dependence on regional assets is not passive. Across time, influential firms also engage with their regional environments to actively build resources, to stimulate a critical mass of firms in their vicinity and to take care of them across time. This is especially the case when technologies are new and require a novel set of resources (Storper & Walker 1989). Few firms can manage to create those on their own. Yet, many firms in more mature industries develop together with their localities too. Because firms collectively shape regional resources, whether they like it or not, firms are – to varying degrees – both "builders" of the regional economic environments and "takers" from it.

Apart from resource creation and use, firms rely on their regions for other reasons too. Regional input–output links (local supplier–buyer relationships) tell one story about why firms in regions, at least to some extent, share economic destinies. Many firms are also dependent on the success of other firms in their region because of demand, and by means of so-called regional multipliers. The local supermarket, restaurant or hairdresser are all dependent on sufficient local demand, and the fact that other firms employ people so that they have money to consume the offered services. Although regional multipliers are also important to understand why the regional lens on the economy makes sense, they will not be explicitly discussed in this book. They are well explained elsewhere (Stutz & Warf 2012) and only have an indirect relationship with regional economic change, the main focus of this book.

Regional economic change and growth: production and productivity

"Economic change" is not an easy concept. One of the most straightforward ways to think about economic change is to consider what firms in regions actually produce, which resources this involves and how production and resource use changes over time (a "productionist" view).

For example, one of the most important changes in recent decades, in many regional economies (at least in the western hemisphere), is the increased importance of different kinds of services, and a relative decline in manufacturing production and employment.

BOX 1.3 GOTHENBURG

Gothenburg (Göteborg) is home to around a million inhabitants in the metropolitan area. It is located on the Swedish west coast, at the mouth of the Göta river. Founded in the early 1600s, Gothenburg developed quickly into a major trading hub and became an important manufacturing centre during the second industrial revolution. Although its most notable historical specialization, shipbuilding, is today completely dismantled, Gothenburg remains the prime location for several Swedish multinationals, such as Volvo Cars, Volvo Trucks and SKF (rolling bearings). The port of Gothenburg is Scandinavia's largest. Although best known as a centre for advanced manufacturing, the city has significant strengths in related advanced business services. Notable R&D investments are being made in the city, for example in electric vehicles and automation. Chalmers Technical University and the University of Gothenburg both conduct research. An AstraZeneca global research hub is located in Gothenburg.

BOX 1.4 BORÅS

Borås is a Swedish town located 60 km inland from Gothenburg, with a population of about 100,000. Historically, it is most famous for its textile industry, which developed into a significant cluster from the 1920s onwards. When the production of clothing was largely offshored in the 1960s, it developed manufacturing techniques for more advanced niche textiles, as well as design, logistics and management functions and materials' research and development. The University of Borås, including the Swedish School of Textiles, is located in Borås and has around 13,000 students. Borås has also specialized in trade and logistics. Despite the fact that the telecom/electronics manufacturer Ericsson has abandoned traditional manufacturing in Borås, product testing and logistics facilities remain there. Volvo Buses also run a production facility in Borås.

The following is a perfect example of regional economic change in our time. Consider Figure 1.1. It shows that the mid-sized Swedish city of Gothenburg (second largest in Sweden) has transformed from being a manufacturing city, where the production of material goods of different kinds (such as rolling bearings, ships and cars) made up a decisive part of the local economy, to a city

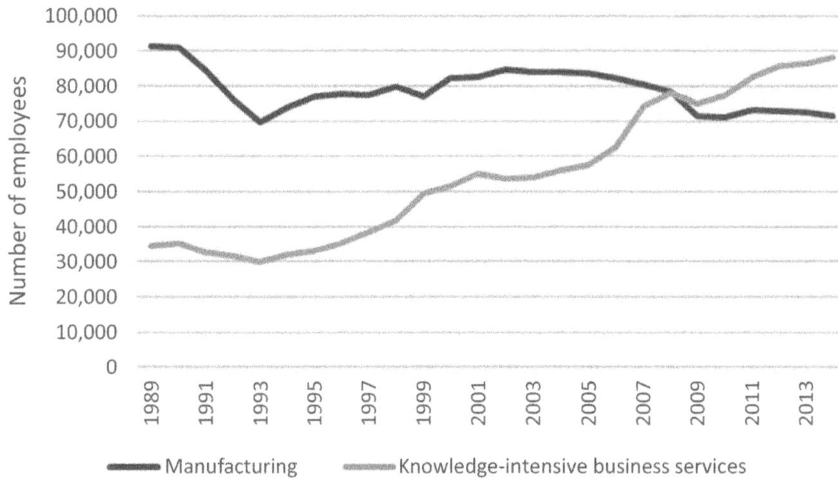

Figure 1.1 Regional economic change in Gothenburg: number of employees in manufacturing and knowledge-intensive business services
Source: own elaborations on data from Statistics Sweden (Henning *et al.* 2017).

where production of services has become much more important, particularly knowledge-intensive producer services. The economic structure of the city has completely changed since the 1970s. The nearby town of Borås experienced a similar change, but it was less drastic (Figure 1.2).

Such a productionist description of deindustrialization captures some of the most important change processes that many regions have experienced in the past decades. This is real economic change, but there are many ways to understand and describe this change. We will return to the processes of regional economic change in Gothenburg and Borås many times in this book. This is not because Gothenburg and Borås are particularly unique: they serve as illustrations of evolutionary processes of economic change that one can find in many regions and cities across the world. Readers can surely identify parallel processes in their own regions, or other regions that they know well.

In the regional literature, it has become common to describe such processes of productionist change along four dimensions:

1. Regional presence of different industries, or produced goods and services (what is actually produced?)
2. Volumes produced or production value in different industries (how much is produced with which type of production?)

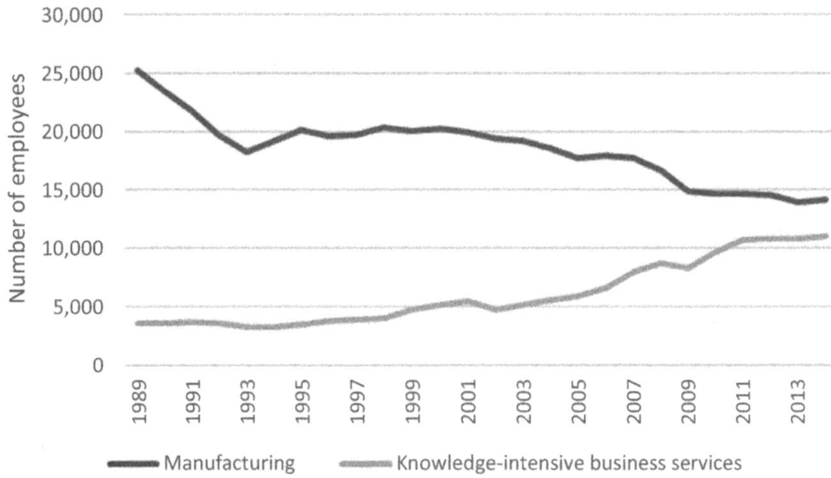

Figure 1.2 Regional economic change in Borås: number of employees in manufacturing and knowledge-intensive business services
Source: own elaborations on data from Statistics Sweden (Henning *et al.* 2017).

3. Amount of regional resources used in production by different industries (which regional resources are being used in production? Employment is by far the most common indicator, as in Figure 1.1)
4. Complexity of the regional economy, measured as the composition of present production, and how unique the products are compared to each other (how does production of various kinds fit together?) (Hidalgo & Hausmann 2009; Gao & Zhou 2018).

Throughout history, product innovation and the production of new innovative products have been important sources of economic change. Yet, original innovation is not everything; diffusion (spread) of production and imitation have been important sources of change too. In other words, regional change in production does not require the products to be entirely novel on a global scale.

The rolling bearing firm, shipyards and vehicle manufacturers in Gothenburg invented many of the key products and technologies that they employ. However, by no means did they invent all the products and technologies that they use. Some of the improvements were completely dependent on what happened in other regions, outside Gothenburg. Innovations and new technologies then spread into Gothenburg, to find new applications there.

Studies of technological diffusion and the spread of industries have a long history of analysis in economic geography. The basic general point is that a region does not need to invent everything to achieve economic change. Over time Gothenburg developed into a great shipbuilding and car production city. However, neither the ship nor the car were invented in Gothenburg, of course. Regional economic change not only takes place because of what happens inside the regions and the resources available there but also because of what happens in other regions.

To evolutionary scholars, with whom we will become acquainted in this book, adding new goods and services to the things that are produced in regions (regional diversification) is the prime link between change and growth. Only those regional economies that diversify can also grow in the longer run. In other words, there is a strong link between economic diversification and wealth (Hidalgo & Hausmann 2009).

BOX 1.5 INNOVATION

Innovation is one of the most widely used concepts in economic geography, and in other economic disciplines too. Although innovation is often used synonymously with discovery, this is normally referred to as an "invention". The Otto engine, which had a great influence on the design of combustion engines, was a typical invention (before it was put into commercial use, which made it a typical "innovation"). The normal use of the concept innovation is both broader and more restricted. First, most scholars tend to think that an important aspect of an innovation is that it is attested by the market. A discovery can become an innovation, but discovery alone is not enough. Second, researchers usually distinguish between product and process innovations (that improve the production processes). Third, there are far more categories of innovations than just technological ones: organizational innovation, market innovation and institutional innovation. As Joseph Schumpeter explained the concept, innovations are "any 'doing things differently' in the realm of economic life" (1939: 84).

Regional economic change can also be considered through a productivity lens. This is close to the productionist view but a little bit different. Productivity improvement is a key factor behind economic growth. Productivity changes can be achieved through capital intensification (using efficient machines instead of labour) but are in practice often linked to technological change.

An increase in productivity is closely linked to the prospects of a region achieving an increased repertoire of produced goods and services. With increased productivity, resources become available and can be put to use in producing other things. However, increased productivity can also be used to take the resources out of production. For example, an entrepreneur can spend an extra hour sleeping on the bench outside the factory, whereas a machine does the job that used to be done manually. There are of course limits to this process, but essentially, human existence has been enormously improved by productivity-improving processes since the 1800s, in terms of material wealth, room for diversification and allowing for a bit more leisure time.

Let us try to summarize this discussion with some more formal definitions in the way they are used in this book. *Regional economic change* is a change in the production of goods and services in a region. It is often accompanied by a change in employment in different industries in a region, and a change in the resources that are used in production. This means that regional economic change is a qualitative process, but one that can be measured quantitatively (this fruitful distinction is not mine but has been made by Frank Neffke). *Increased productivity* means that more output (goods or services) or products of higher value are produced with equal or less input of labour, for example. *Regional growth* measures a change in the volume of goods or services produced.

In this book, we assume the productionist view and explore how the repertoire of production in regions changes over time, and which resources these changes involve. However, these changes are conditional on productivity: if a change results in productivity losses in a region, we cannot call it a productive regional economic change.

Later in this book, we explore how regional economic change in production or productivity does not happen automatically. Change is primarily achieved through a process of regional resource building, resource use and improvement of regional resources, as well as through trade with other regions. Nevertheless, someone has to achieve these processes; they are neither automatic nor mechanical. In a term frequently used by a growing literature, achieving productive change requires "agency" (Grillitsch & Sotarauta 2020).

At times, one can observe that scholars prefer the term "regional economic development" to reflect how regions progress in economic terms. It is sometimes hard to explain what scholars exactly mean by this. One interpretation that comes very close is that they mean economic change with a productive outcome; in essence, positive change. Development implies that something gets better, at least on average. Yet, understanding regional economic change not only involves understanding how things get better but also when and how things go wrong.

Regional divergence, development and policy

Contrary to conventional expectations, the fact that regions develop different economic specialties, become increasingly integrated during globalization and adopt a market-based ideology has not, at least so far, reduced the overall economic differences between regions within countries. On the contrary, the differences between regions within countries today are huge, albeit at a higher level of development than before. In many countries, regional differences are in fact far greater now than they were in 1980 (Rosés & Wolf 2018).

In the long term, increasing economic differences between regions is a dangerous thing. When observable economic differences increase, the risk that social and political tensions will increase becomes higher. The "geography of discontent" in both Europe and North America is a cause of growing concern to policy-makers and scientists alike (Rodríguez-Pose 2018). This discussion provides important lessons for an analysis of economic change. It again highlights that an average, positive regional economic change can nevertheless be destructive to some individuals and some regions. When changes in production are not matched with an overall positive change in productivity, the result can be that some people in some regions actually become worse off than they were before. It is very important to understand also how such a malign scenario can be a partial outcome of economic change too.

In response to this and many other concerns, governments and other organizations (like the European Union (EU)) spend vast amounts of money on overcoming differences in economic fortunes between regions, and reinforcing the positive aspects of economic change. While much can be left to the markets, some degree of government intervention seems justified. Much is being spent on building regional resources to achieve productive change or mediating the negative outcomes of economic changes that threaten to become detrimental. Around the globe, policy-makers work to promote their specific region.

For example, regional policy is second only to agriculture when it comes to EU expenditure. The aim of reducing regional disparities and promoting economic cohesion is even engraved in the very statutes of the Union (Lisbon Treaty, Article 174), where, in the words of the European Commission: "Economic and social cohesion – as defined in the 1986 Single European Act – is about 'reducing disparities between the various regions and the backwardness of the least-favoured regions'" (EU n.d.a.).

This all means that for a long time, policy-makers have considered geography important. So far, however, it is obvious that much remains to be achieved when it comes to reducing regional disparities. Substantial differences in welfare remain, not only between states but also within regions (Rosés & Wolf 2018).

In recent years, many academics and policy-makers have found that a long-term view of economic change has helped them to understand how regions change and grow across time and how regional policy should address that. For example, the EU's "smart specialization" initiative is one of many regional policy frameworks that aim to promote constructive change and growth in specific localities and it incorporates an explicit time perspective (Foray 2014).

In the last couple of years, regions across Europe have been working to come up with smart specialization strategies to access (parts of) European regional policy funding. Explaining the framework, the Commission states:

> Smart specialisation is about identifying the unique characteristics and assets of each country and region, highlighting each region's competitive advantages, and rallying regional stakeholders and resources around an excellence-driven vision of their future. It also means strengthening regional innovation systems, maximising knowledge flows and spreading the benefits of innovation throughout the entire regional economy.
>
> (European Commission 2014, bold sections in original source revised)

An interesting aspect of regional specialization is its view on qualitative change in regional economies. Again, in the words of the Commission: "The most promising way for a region to promote its knowledge-based growth is to diversify into technologies, products and services that are closely related to existing dominant technologies and the regional skills base" (European Commission 2014).

This means that smart specialization builds on theoretical ideas that come very close to many discussions in this book that precisely deal with how to describe existing technologies and the regional skills base, how specializations develop over longer periods of time, the principles of regional diversification and who introduces novelty in regional economies (but also what stalls change). Therefore, this book gives a background to much of the logical reasoning that underpins the ideas of modern smart specialization and other knowledge-driven regional policy approaches for productive long-run regional economic change.

The outline of the book

We begin by exploring the two fundamental literatures that provide a base for the rest of the book: evolutionary economic geography (Chapter 2) and time geography (Chapter 3). After that, we start to develop some core arguments from these literatures further, in order to understand regional economic change in a globalized economy better.

Chapters 4, 5 and 6 develop the details of an "evolutionary perspective" to show how the production of manufactured products and services takes place. This perspective is based on recent evolutionary research, and a regional extension of the resource-based view of the firm. The basic ideas are not new to geography, but the chapters spell out some details that have not been thoroughly discussed before. Examples are drawn from Gothenburg and Borås. Again, the details of these particular examples are not important but the overall lessons from them are.

Chapters 7 and 8 continue to explore what goes on within regions in terms of economic activities, and how this links to evolutionary economic change. Chapter 7 introduces concepts and methods to distinguish and measure different kinds of change and how regional path dependency occurs through chains of related diversification. Chapter 8 discusses co-location of economic activities – agglomerations – and how they prepare for different types of change. The properties of places affect the types of change that are likely to happen there.

However, there is one great problem with the evolutionary perspective in economic geography: it does not adequately take into account the secular changes in communication costs, transportation costs and institutional changes that have resulted in globalization. Therefore, Chapters 9 and 10 use the tools that time geography provides to explore how regional evolutionary economic change happens in a globalized economy. We find that globalization revolutionized the ways in which regions change. Chapter 11 concludes the book with a short summary and some lessons for regional policy.

Discussion points

1. Consider how your grandparents or great-grandparents lived their lives. Are you better off in a material sense? Try to explain why/why not.
2. How important is economic change when it comes to explaining social and political movements in your region (such as changes in income inequality and political party preferences)? Does this call for political action?
3. How has globalization changed your region?
4. Is regional economic policy needed? Are there aspects other than economic ones that justify regional economic policies?

2

Evolutionary economic geography

> In our evolutionary approach to economic geography, we start from the definition of economic geography as dealing with the uneven distribution of economic activity across space. An evolutionary approach specifically focuses on the historical processes that produce these patterns.
>
> R. Boschma & K. Frenken, "The emerging empirics of evolutionary economic geography", 296

Evolutionary economic geography: how and why regional economies change across time

Some of the main ideas that this book explores are: how regional resources condition the specialization and future direction of change in regional economies (some call them "paths"); and how, with globalization, resources readily imported from other regions fundamentally influence how economic change happens. As we know, the conditioning of economic change on space and time may have positive as well as negative outcomes. The economic histories of regions enable, as much as they restrict, change. History is a mixed blessing.

Evolutionary research into regional economies provides an intellectual backdrop, or theoretical basis, to such ideas. Recent research has uncovered a great deal about how long-term regional economic change and regional growth actually happens (Boschma & Frenken 2006; Boschma & Martin 2010). The evolutionary economic geography approach works in the tradition of the Austro-American economist Joseph Schumpeter, and it recognizes innovation, technological change and the diffusion of technologies as the most important drivers behind economic change and growth. In essence, evolutionary theories work from the basic assumption that firm competition takes place in free markets, and that the economy operates under the normal institutional structures that characterize liberal market economy modes of governance. However, there is plenty to be said about the relationships between the role of government and economic evolution, and we return to this throughout the book. Even if we assume that competition is something that concerns firms in liberal markets, this does not mean that markets can provide all regional resources, nor that markets will work without regulation.

BOX 2.1 JOSEPH SCHUMPETER

Joseph Schumpeter (1883–1950) is famous for his ideas about "creative destruction". Schumpeter regarded innovation, entrepreneurship and market competition on the basis of innovations as core processes for economic evolution and growth. For Schumpeter and his followers, economic development is always twofold – involving the creation of new structures based on new technologies and processes and the necessary phasing out of the old and obsolete ones (Schumpeter 1911). Schumpeter also contributed to the study of "long waves" of economic development, where he noted how distinctly different periods of great technological shifts can be compared to periods characterized by slower change and development (Schumpeter 1939). There are several distinct phases to Schumpeter's work, but the "early Schumpeter" has remained one of the main sources of inspiration for economic geographers in general, and for evolutionary economic geographers in particular.

It is important to note that the evolutionary focus is not without complications. There are many competing and complementing approaches to this particular view of economic change, or at least to where it places its emphasis. Yet, much recent regional research has found value in the "neo-Schumpeterian" view.

To summarize the idea of evolutionary economic geography, Ron Boschma and Ron Martin have explained that the main concern of evolutionary economic geography is "the processes by which the economic landscape – the spatial organization of economic production, circulation, exchange, distribution and consumption – is transformed from within over time" (Boschma & Martin 2010: 6). Also:

> EEG [evolutionary economic geography] is concerned with the spatialities of economic novelty ... , with how the spatial structures of the economy emerge from the micro-behaviours of economic agents ... ; with how ... the economic landscape exhibits self-organization; and with and how the processes of path creation and path dependence interact to shape geographies of economic development and transformation, and why and how such processes may themselves be place dependent. (Boschma & Martin 2010: 7)

In our terminology, evolutionary economic geography is a perspective interested in the processes of regional economic change, how they work and how they are conditioned by space and time. So far, the evolutionary framework has been especially helpful in trying to answer questions such as:

- How and why the geographical location of economic activities (such as industries and firms) changes across time;
- How established regional resources (such as labour, infrastructure or institutions) condition economic change;
- How regional resources develop over time to accommodate economic change;
- What the most important agents (introducers) of economic change are and which ones seem to stall change;
- When regional economic change is creative and when it is destructive; and
- What the consequences of regional economic change are to firms and individuals.

BOX 2.2 REGIONAL INSTITUTIONS

The role of regional institutions is a topic of debate in evolutionary economic geography. Formal institutions are, for example, laws upheld by official authorities. Regional informal institutions are, for example, regional attitudes, norms or patterns of acceptable behaviour. In the evolutionary literature in geography, there has been some debate around regional informal institutions and how they influence economic change. However, adjacent literatures, for example those that can be counted as "institutional economic geography", have spent decades investigating this issue. It is clear that informal institutions differ between regions (norms vary). Most evolutionary scholars would also recognize that regional institutions influence patterns of regional change. However, some evolutionary scholars have been sceptical of institutions and their effect on evolutionary processes in regional economies, because institutions are notoriously hard to measure and they are merely part of more complex explanations for regional change and cannot be assumed to have the same effects in different contexts. Attitudes are changing, and so are the data. Recent contributions show how much common ground there is between evolutionary and institutional economic geography. Therefore, the framework that we work with in this book also considers regional institutions, although maybe not at the level of detail that devoted institutional economic geographers think is necessary. See Boschma & Frenken (2009) and Trippl *et al.* (2020).

In analysing these different questions, the evolutionary approach develops many different subtleties and varieties. The literature is diverse when it comes to the methods and materials used, and the different topics they cover. In addition, scholars have suggested that much previous research in economic geography and economic history was empirically "evolutionary" in essence, long before the concept itself was coined. Notwithstanding these previous efforts, the systematization of evolutionary ideas and the development of a more coherent terminology around them is a recent phenomenon.

There has been considerable debate about whether evolutionary economics and evolutionary economic geography really are "evolutionary" in the "Darwinian" sense, whether they should be and what that would actually mean for modern economic research. This debate is very theoretical and is something that does not need further exploration in this book. Overall, it is fair to say that the most recent versions of evolutionary economic geography are a long way from Darwin in a formal sense. Work in evolutionary economic geography has, in practice, accommodated theories and a wide range of research methodologies from innovation studies, entrepreneurship, industrial dynamics and traditional economic geography, to explain the change of regional economies and long-term regional growth. However, the evolutionary literature is certainly inspired by analogies from evolutionary biology.

Even within this diversity of evolutionary contributions, there is a common theoretical core that evolutionary economic scholars seem to accept either explicitly or implicitly. In its essence, the core ideas of evolutionary economic geography can be captured in three concepts that build the evolutionary notion around regional economic change: novelty, retention and selection (Essletzbichler & Rigby 2010). We explore these concepts (Figure 2.1) to

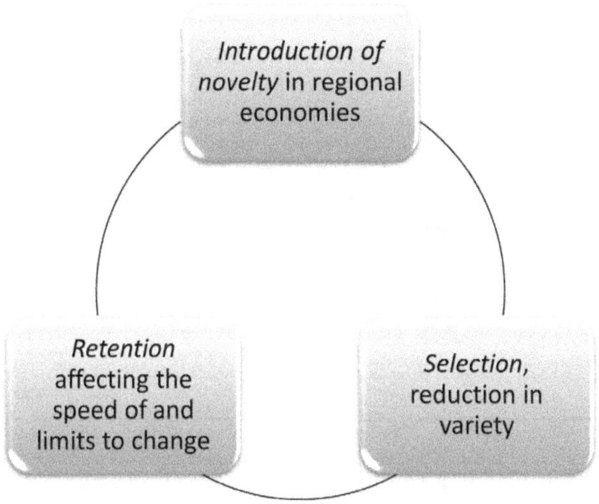

Figure 2.1 The core concepts of evolutionary economic change
Source: based on Essletzbichler & Rigby (2010).

understand how evolutionary economic geography sets about developing its approach to regional economic change.

Novelty, diversification and evolution

To achieve sustained growth, elements of novelty need to be regularly introduced into regional economies. This idea reflects the position of Boschma and Martin that evolutionary economic geography takes its point of departure from the "spatialities of economic novelty". It also reflects the ideas of Schumpeter about the importance of innovations.

First, consider an economic novelty such as a new manufacturing good or service being produced in a region: a product novelty. This could reflect the regional application of a product innovation, such as firms inventing a new product, based on their own development work, and then producing it in the region. The multinational firm SKF, based in Gothenburg, that produces rolling bearings started in exactly that way. The engineer Sven Wingquist found a solution to an industrial production problem by inventing a particular type of rolling bearing. This innovation became the foundation both of new production in Gothenburg and of one of Sweden's most important multinationals.

BOX 2.3 INTRODUCTION OF NOVELTIES IN REGIONS

The study into how novelties are introduced in regions is challenging, especially in the service sectors. In many economies data sources include patents, occupations, products and industries. Because exact data on goods and services produced in regions are often hard to come by, many evolutionary geographers take a shortcut and study production novelties and diversification as the establishment of new industries in regions. Obviously, this means studying diversification on an aggregate level. See Neffke, Henning & Boschma (2011), Boschma, Minondo & Navarro (2013) and Boschma, Balland & Kogler (2015).

The invention that is put into productive use in a region does not have to originate in that same region to give rise to regional product novelty. For example, Volvo's introduction of car making to Gothenburg in 1927 was an economic novelty to the region. No one had made cars there before. Car production proved to be a long-lasting affair, but the car itself was of course not invented in Gothenburg.

Although some innovations are important for incremental changes in production processes and for increasing productivity marginally, some create new industries and change the course of history (Freeman, Clark & Soete 1982). The combustion engine (Otto engine) is one example of a grand innovation that provided scope for many more and complementary production novelties in regions. In practice, most product innovations are incremental and have limited impact. Nonetheless, they can be important sources of regional economic novelties. Therefore, for the study of regional change, not only is innovation important, it also becomes important to know how innovations diffuse, or spread, through different areas and introduce novelties to an expanding number of regional economies.

Car makers, such as Volvo in Gothenburg, have tweaked the performance and efficiency of combustion engines into almost endless productive novelties, many of them providing a competitive basis for their respective models. Such "mutations" and cross-combinations have, for example, resulted in far more fuel-efficient combustion engines over time. Automakers have developed numerous complementary innovations and, added together, this has resulted in a (so far) never-ending stream of regional production novelties in the car industry.

Economic novelty also comes through as process innovations, and economic history provides many examples of how complementary organizational innovations, such as new ways of organizing production, are needed to make the most of product novelties. Product and process innovations are often intertwined.

In sum, evolutionary economic geography recognizes the mutual dependence of different kinds of innovations, especially as regions grow more entrenched in their specializations over time. Yet, the emphasis in terms of economic novelty still lies firmly with products and diversification, rather than other kinds of novelty such as production process improvements. In economists' language, evolutionary scholars care more about products and variety than productivity. In practice though, product and process novelty often become inseparable.

It should also be mentioned that some definitions of innovation require a completely new product/process, whereas others settle with the requirement of them being new to, for example, a regional economy. In this book, we accept the latter and primarily take interest in product innovations that result in productive novelties within a region.

In the wider evolutionary literature, and certainly in the early works of evolutionary economic geography, there used to be a much stronger organizational focus, where research concentrated on novelty in terms of firm routines (Nelson & Winter 1982; Boschma & Frenken 2006). According to our definition, routines are the established schemes of action that firms use when they produce and take decisions about production. These change over time, but whether firm routines are outcomes of almost automated schemes of action, or schemes that are actively chosen and changed, is debatable (Brauer & Laamanen 2014). It is possible to find examples of both in most firms, but it is also possible that change in routines is conditioned by past organizational experiences. Yet, of course, firm routines are frequently deliberately changed. If they were not, it would be hard to explain the existence of organizational innovations that introduce new routines to firms.

In practice, the applied literature on evolutionary economic geography has not made much out of the issue of organizational routines. Rather, it has pursued a more general idea about novelty in the form of new production and technologies. Organizational routines are often complementary but latent (hidden or unobserved) aspects that help to explain why production novelties form the basis for regional economic change. This book follows that path.

Retention and evolution

Whereas novelty and diversification in regional economies symbolize the prospects for future growth, change does not occur in a random direction.

Retention captures the idea that there are mechanisms that tend to slow economic change down, and in some cases even prevent it. Importantly, from an evolutionary point of view, this also indicates that change cannot proceed in just any direction. It is difficult for a regional economy to go from specializing in traditional manufacturing to one specialized in biotech. That is of course an extreme example, but it shows that history, or rather what has happened in the past and the choices made, strongly influences the alternatives for regional change that are available at certain points in time.

Traditional economic geography also deploys a (rather restricted) term for cases when industries are located at sites that reflected past optimal locations rather than present ones: inertia. Inertia is the result of large investments having been made into a particular location that makes relocation to a new, optimal site unfeasible.

In the evolutionary economic literature, the historical factors that explain retention have more to do with the different qualities of investments made than their direct costs (although they sometimes go hand in hand). Cases where previous regional economic structures and decisions clearly condition the economic opportunities of regions are often referred to as regional path dependency (Fuchs & Shapira 2005; Martin & Sunley 2006; Martin 2010). Theories about path dependency, many of which are "evolutionary", explain why retention is an important concept for understanding how regional economic change happens (or does not happen).

The most common examples of path dependency come from the history of technology. They explain why certain standards, which subsequently become inefficient, persist. The most iconic example is the awkward QWERTY keyboard that endures despite the fact that the mechanical hurdles making it necessary have long since been overcome (David 1985). For computerized keyboards, there are few sensible arguments for keeping the QWERTY keyboard. Yet, at some point so many things are adapted to a particular standard that it becomes difficult and costly to change it.

Regional (evolutionary) interpretations of path dependency are similar in spirit to the iconic technological examples of path dependency, but the logics are not exactly the same. Regional applications normally focus on the direction of change and how this becomes reinforced over time: "path dependence specifically addresses the sequence of historic development paths and how path dependence can be viewed as a process defining an ever-narrowing window of available choices" (Henning, Stam & Wenting 2013: 1351).

This relates to principles of irreversibility. Once a choice about a particular economic change has been made, reinforcing mechanisms kick in that make it hard to reverse the processes and make it hard to shift the direction of change.

By far the best analogy to illustrate this is to picture regional economic change as a tree diagram or "branching process" (Frenken & Boschma 2007). Along a branch, there are many factors in regions that slow change and even make some economic choices impossible. Selecting one path, for example by investing and starting to produce a certain product in a region, will probably lead to other possibilities in the future. However, it also means that other potential products or technologies are not pursued. As regional assets and ways of thinking are adapted to the selected path over time, it becomes increasingly difficult to switch to a different type of production. At the extreme, this results in a lock-in of the economic structure of the region, at which point it becomes extremely hard to redirect it (Grabher 1993).

A typical example of this is how a region's labour force is shaped and develops over time. People are trained in specific skills, and often over time gain practical experience from working with those skills in a specific field. Once the labour force in a region becomes specialized in certain fields, it becomes increasingly difficult to transfer to completely different industries or to make completely different types of products.

This means that taking a particular path is a mixed blessing: it involves the virtues of specialization but also closing down alternative opportunities. Nevertheless, past resource investment decisions cannot easily be undone.

Economic retention is central to the explanation of varieties of change in regional economic structures. If it were not for retention, regional economies would adapt more quickly to changing circumstances and to the wishes of the market, especially in a global economy where geographical distance matters less than before. Because of the mechanisms of retention, both time and place are still important to economic change.

Now, if path-dependent processes and retention are so important that they may even dominate how much regional economic change occurs, it also becomes important to ask in what ways new production paths actually develop in regions or, in the terminology of the literature, how paths "are created" (Karnøe & Garud 2012; MacKinnon *et al.* 2019). This is an essential mechanism in the evolutionary view of economies, and something that we will return to, because with globalization, mechanisms behind both path creation and regional path dependency have changed.

Selection and evolution

There is constant pressure on regions to reduce their production repertoire: in other words, to reduce the economic variety that innovation has precipitated.

The third core process in the evolutionary approach to economic change is selection.

The introduction of economic novelty is an experiment. Forces selecting production candidates counterbalance the expansion of economic variety produced by novelty, which would otherwise be endless. The selection process decides which technologies, products, firms and industries are allowed to survive and grow in the regional economy on the one hand, and which ones have to disappear, on the other.

The easiest answer to how selection mechanisms work would be: costs. Traditionally, however, evolutionary scholars and scholars concerned with regional clusters do not have a very intimate relationship with price theory and costs. Admittedly, much evolutionary geography research about regional development has for the most part left price dynamics out of the picture, as a latent (unobserved) factor that influences the variety of goods and services that regions offer. Scholars relied on the observation of realized production as an indicator of a region being able to offer a good or service at a competitive price to the market.

The most obvious price logic from an evolutionary point of view is therefore the following: as markets act as selection environments for competing producers and goods, producers need to supply their goods to a market at competitive prices. This will affect the resource (input) cost that a producer is willing to carry and the final decision made to produce a good or a service, redirect the use of an input or let them lie idle (not to take up or close down production).

BOX 2.4 THE INDUSTRY/PRODUCT LIFE CYCLE

The industry/product life cycle is often used by evolutionary economic geographers to illustrate how the characteristics of an industry or a product, its demand patterns and its best production locations change across time and with processes of technological maturity. There are many versions of the cycle in the literature, but the basic ones distinguish between phases of introduction, growth, maturity, decline and obsolescence. During the cycle, the main innovation efforts shift from product to process innovation, and the competitive logics from product to price competition. However, the sequence of the life cycle of an industry or a product is not deterministic. After phases of maturity, for example, industries may experience renewal, which results in a new growth phase. This goes for products too – technological change might broaden the application of a product and therefore extend its life cycle. See Klepper (1996) and Neffke *et al.* (2011).

The industry and product life cycle theories provide clues as to how prices of regional resources, and the willingness of firms to pay these costs, change as firms and industries progress (Lundquist 1996; Neffke *et al.* 2011). According to this logic, the costs of doing production in a region will be especially determined by: (1) costs for using resources, including procurement, which encompasses remuneration for the creation of the resource as well as communication costs; (2) economies of scale and scope in the firms; and (3) cost savings made possible by the co-location of firms.

BOX 2.5 ECONOMIES OF SCALE AND SCOPE

Economies of scale are cost savings made by producing more units of something, resulting in a lower production cost per unit. In the case of chair manufacturing, regardless of how many chairs you want to produce, you still have to invest in certain tools, machines and materials. If you produce lots of chairs, you will be able to distribute those costs across a higher number of chairs. Per chair, this will decrease the production costs. Higher levels of production will also enable workers to specialize, thus becoming more efficient on parts of the production sequence. Economies of scope are cost savings made by producing certain products together. When producing the chairs, the factory could use the time in between the different production stages and the existing tools and machines to produce other kinds of furniture too. It might also obtain procurement discounts for material, such as wood. In this case, the average production costs of the chairs would be lower as they would for the other furniture. Economies of scope and scale can be both internal (within the firm) and external (through the collaboration between several firms, e.g. in a region). More about this in Chapter 8.

If we combine the life cycle theories with evolutionary economic geography, there are three different, time-dependent processes that capture how selection is linked to production costs over time:

1. *Product cycle.* As a product or industry ages, and market demand diminishes towards the end of the life cycle, it will prove hard to achieve economies of scale or scope. The typewriter is a perfect example: a great innovation in its day but now an uncompetitive product. The production of typewriters is likely to be deselected from regional economies: they have become too expensive for their purpose compared to the alternatives.

2. *Process development.* A specific type of production in a region may be outcompeted by producers in other regions because of price or quality concerns, even though the product itself is not technologically obsolete in the wider market. Nevertheless, the result is the deselection of that production from the regional repertoire. The offshoring of manufacturing activities from Europe, the USA or Canada to lower-cost countries during globalization is an example of this. With their current process setup, many firms could not continue to justify locating certain types of manufacturing in the industrialized countries, considering the lower wages in competing economies. This resulted in an "offshoring" of production. Now there is speculation that innovation will reverse this trend in the longer run, as automation enables low-cost production processes in high-wage countries ("reshoring"), and as some firms have experienced coordination problems involved in offshoring production. So far, however, there is not much real evidence of this reversal.
3. *Opportunity costs.* Regional resources used for production are not endless. At times, the regional assets used in one type of production may become more attractive to use in other types of production. Certainly, many firms in Gothenburg could survive by making other kinds of products than the ones they actually do. However, after a long chain of decisions, they have ended up with a particular production repertoire that is currently the best alternative, or is at least good enough. Selecting to produce a certain good or service also involves deselecting alternatives. Prices for sought-after regional resources will also increase, stimulating local producers to use them in the most productive way that they can conceive of.

Selection is part of daily economic life. Nevertheless, it can of course have a great impact on individuals and communities. The speed of this selection process, or indeed the reduction of variety in a regional economy, varies greatly across time. During good times, selection is slow and incremental. During economic crises, selection can place an enormous pressure on regional economies, as drops in demand deselect entire ranges of products. At times, this may even result in the loss of whole industries, and their exit from a region can have devastating consequences. For example, a series of dramatic shipyard closures during the 1970s and 1980s in Gothenburg resulted in the complete dismantling of shipbuilding in this once proud and world-renowned shipbuilding city.

Process innovations of course also affect production costs and, therefore, selection. In Sweden, as in many other countries, a wide range of process innovations have increased labour productivity drastically in the manufacturing industries across recent decades. This has contributed to a reduction in employment in this sector to a fraction of what it used to be 30 years ago. At the same time, Swedish manufacturing is producing the same or even greater volumes than it used to. Through product and process innovation, elements of manufacturing have survived even in countries and regions with very high labour costs, such as Sweden.

In practice, it is difficult to make a clear distinction between product and process innovations. They are often linked to each other, whereby process novelty underpins product novelty in regions.

So far, we have implicitly assumed that selection takes place as a market process. Looking at history, it becomes clear that this is not always the case. An economic selection always has to be made, however. Resources are not endless. Under some institutional settings, individuals and agencies – such as planners, economists or politicians (and not the market) – will make the selection. To a varying extent across countries and time, this was the case in the socialist command economies of eastern Europe until the early 1990s.

Also in the economies that we tend to think of as market economies, there are infinite varieties in the ways that selection processes are organized. Markets are of course important and are the main selection agents. At times though, states may step in and intervene in the selection process, for environmental, public health or national security reasons. Therefore, we cannot assume that market forces always dominate real selection in real economies.

Finally, there is still the tricky question of what is actually selected. Clearly, it is easiest to think of selection in terms of products (both services and physical goods). As consumers and firms make choices about which products to buy (based on its attributes and price), the products that fulfil the requirements are chosen for continued production in regional economies. Others are deselected. This is a simple and straightforward explanation of market selection.

In the real world, selection permeates the entire production process: it is not just a final issue for the end producer and end customer. Producers select the inputs that are available from different suppliers. They also weigh labour inputs against using capital (process setup) and make a selection regarding which resources to use. Selection permeates all tiers of the value chain of goods and services on the way to the final consumer. The multiple selection processes along the value-creating process results in a particular product setup, which is finally selected by a market. The "market" only makes the final selection in a long chain of selection processes.

A global perspective on regional economic evolution

From an evolutionary point of view, regional economic prosperity is a delicate balance between the introduction of novelty, variation and selection. If the selection and reduction of variety is not counterbalanced by the introduction of novelty and economic variety, a region will enter an economic downward spiral. There is a constant pressure and need for renewal; sometimes this is incremental, but at times it is drastic and radical. In the economic crisis of Gothenburg in the 1970s and 1980s, workers and politicians had to find new alternatives quickly for the people who had to leave the city's big shipyards, but they also had to identify new alternatives for future generations of workers in Gothenburg for when the shipyards were no longer active. On average, they actually succeeded.

In the rest of the book, we explore some of the most important mechanisms of regional change in our time. From a theoretical point of view, this requires an expansion of some aspects of evolutionary economic geography.

First, evolutionary economic geography has not yet managed to explain the link between routines at firm level, regional resources, the production based on these resources and regional path dependency. The early evolutionary attempts that focused on connections between firm routines and geography did not get around to that, and never established a comprehensive regional "perspective" that could explain the ways in which the constitution of the regional economic environment also conditions future economic change. (Also, it has not connected to earlier research on firms in economic geography; Taylor & Ashiem 2001; Maskell 2001.)

However, recent developments promise a great deal. Evolutionary scholars have already started to develop some generalized ideas about regional resources and capabilities, and how they condition (enable and constrain) regional economic change (Neffke *et al.* 2018). Many of these arguments about the resource bases of regions are not new, but the systematization of different views from the strategy literature and geography, consistent with evolutionary economic geography, is new.

This book builds on this work and further develops an evolutionary perspective of regional production and change, which is now largely implicit in disparate parts of the literature. This is the focus of Chapters 4–8.

Second, as we saw in the first Chapter 1, a regional evolutionary theory for our time needs to incorporate the impact of economic globalization on the introduction of novelty, retention and selection in regional economies. We take a step towards that in Chapter 3 and then return to the issue in Chapters 9 and 10.

Some will undoubtedly think that the evolutionary perspective suggested here, and the theories that accompany it, are far too general: the wide variety of regional inputs and its variety of uses in different industries can surely not be collapsed into one aggregate evolutionary perspective or worldview of regional resources, services and capabilities. The intention of this book is to focus on the characteristics that different regional resources and services share, rather than what makes them different. This evolutionary perspective deals with the regional production of goods and services, how it happens and how it conditions the future.

Evolutions, relations and time

Evolutionary economic geography is of course not the only approach that scholars have developed to make sense of how regional economies develop in our time. For example, and perhaps most importantly, Harald Bathelt and Johannes Glückler at the beginning of the 2000s argued that a "relational economic geography" revolves around four "-ions": organization, evolution, innovation and interaction (Bathelt & Glückler 2003).

By many accounts, these scholars are of course completely right: economic geography and the development of regions during globalization is about relations and the different "-ions". Relational economic geography and evolutionary economic geography also share some fundamental interests in time, evolution, regional path dependency and innovation. Some of its basis for inspiration, such as the works by Michael Storper, Richard Nelson and Sidney Winter, is also the same.

However, evolutionary economic geography has come to stress formalized testing, traditional causal analysis and path dependency sequences more in its empirical applications. In a sense, evolutionary economic geography is the more "productionist" of the two. Relational economic geography, on the other hand, considers geographical context in a qualitatively more profound way, and provides the means to analyse the impact of relations between regions more effectively than evolutionary economic geography.

Unfortunately, the two approaches never quite meet, neither theoretically nor empirically. This book of course leans heavily towards evolutionary economic geography but with the acknowledgement that a relational economic geography has, and could, bring much to the table to expand the evolutionary view. In fact, the author of this book is looking forward to the future merger of evolutionary economic geography and relational economic geography, much to the benefit of our understanding about how regional economies change over time!

Discussion points

1. Why are regional economic change and growth interesting topics for research?
2. From an economic point of view, what is a region? What delimits it?

3. Consider your everyday physical environment. What evidence of the economic past can you identify? What does this tell you about how and when regional industries were competitive, and the various ways in which people tried to make a living?
4. Consider the products (things) around you. Where were they made? What does this tell us about the globalization of economic production?

3

Time geography

> [T]ime has a critical importance when it comes to fitting people and things together for functioning in social-economic systems, whether these undergo long-term changes, or rest in something which could be defined as a steady state. What I have in mind is the introduction of a time-space concept which could help us to develop a kind of a socio-economic web model.
>
> T. Hägerstrand, "What about people in regional science?", 145.

Space and time

Improved means of communication and the liberalization of trade, resulting in globalization, has profoundly altered how regions link to each other. Such an empirical insight is of course trivial, but it is not as easy to understand how globalization has affected the ways that economic change in particular plays out in regional economies. So far, evolutionary economic geography has, with a few exceptions, refrained from integrating its ideas about novelty, retention and selection in regional economies with globalization.

In order to be relevant today and explain how regions change and grow in our time, the ideas of evolutionary economic geography need to be combined with a framework that allows us to explore and explain exactly how lower-cost and faster communications have transformed regional novelty, retention and selection processes in an era of globalization. In this chapter, we investigate whether "time geography" can provide such a framework (Hägerstrand 1991; Pred 1977). Although time geography has not frequently been used to answer research questions in economic geography, it has recently enjoyed something of a revived interest in transport geography (Neutens, Schwanen & Witlox

2011; Ellegård & Svedin 2012) and at the intersection between human geography and gender studies (Scholten, Friberg & Sandén 2012).

The Swedish geographer Torsten Hägerstrand published the first papers about time geography in the early 1970s. Time geography focuses on individuals, how they move in space and over time, how people meet to accomplish projects and how people's movements are constrained by different identifiable factors. Hägerstrand never developed his time geography into a theory about economic production by explaining how "fitting people together" in space and time is (was) a necessary condition for the production of goods and services (Hägerstrand 1970). However, Hägerstrand came close to accomplishing this before he left economic geography to venture into other fields of research.

Hägerstrand's time geography should be interpreted as a reaction to the highly stylized mathematically archaic approach to economic geography that dominated Western economic geography during much of the 1960s and 1970s. This economic geography provided little room for real people and institutions. When Hägerstrand discussed flows in time-space domains (areas), he therefore argued that: "I think it is true to say that the system of domains is much better understood with respect to flows of goods and money than with respect to flows of people" (Hägerstrand 1970: 152). Thus, Hägerstrand started out with people but did not rule out that "things" also have time-space coordinates and need to be coordinated to produce a specific outcome or, in time geography terminology, to accomplish a project.

This chapter explores time geography ideas using the same concepts and sequence that Hägerstrand himself used in a speech to the Regional Science Association in 1970 (Hägerstrand 1970).

Coordination of people and things

The basic idea of time geography is to provide a set of tools and a theoretical framework to analyse how people and things are able, required and allowed to move in space across time. Time geography is both a method and an approach that allows individuals to have coordinates (or positions) not just in space as on an ordinary map but in time-space. Hägerstrand even argued that the time-space coordination of "people and things" is fundamental to how society works, and understanding how this coordination takes place requires "a kind of a socio-economic web model" (Hägerstrand 1970: 145).

The basic methodological idea formulated by Hägerstrand was that the spatial movements of individuals can be depicted in a time-space diagram as a "choreographic path". In the extreme, this will be the life path of an individual from the time and location of her birth to the time and location at her death, via a great number of time-location coordinates during her life span. The time-space diagram is scalable both in terms of geography and time; one could look at a specific daily path too, and on a range of geographical scales, from the micro-geography of a home to regions or even countries. Figure 3.1 describes a simple path of an individual during a specified time (say, a day) over space. Let us imagine a worker travelling from home to work, and then home via a substantial visit to the chess club or the pub (depending on one's preferences).

Individual paths in time-space are not constructed at random. Indeed, the movement of people and things in time-space is, with a modern term that we now recognize, path dependent. Establishing paths in time-space induces path dependency, because, as Hägerstrand himself put it: "'somewhere' is always critically tied to the 'somewhere' of a moment earlier" (Hägerstrand 1970: 145).

Individuals meet in time-space in order to create specific projects. Hägerstrand named these meetings "bundles", which are formed in order to produce, consume, transact (Hägerstrand 1970).

In the example in Figure 3.1, the individual is likely to participate in two bundles: at work and at the chess club (or the pub). The bundles are formed with colleagues at work and with the opponents and friends at the chess club (alternatively, with the drinking fellows in the pub). The purpose of the

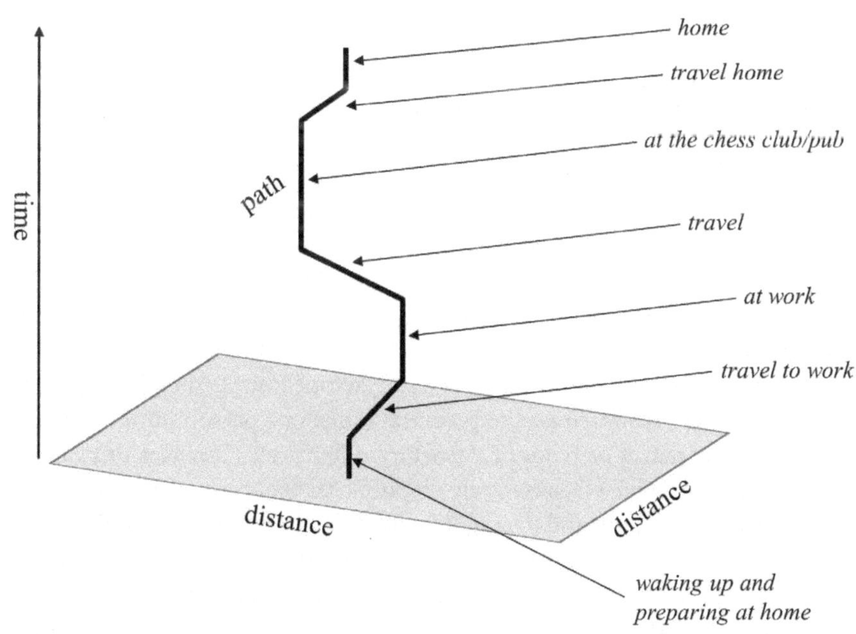

Figure 3.1 A daily path
Source: author's drawing based on Hägerstrand (1970: 148).

projects that presuppose the bundles (getting people together in time-space) is to produce (at work), transact (at the chess club) or consume (in the pub).

Subsequent research following the time geography tradition often stresses how forming the bundles requires the coordination of individuals in time-space. This is true, but Hägerstrand also acknowledged that bundles often involves coordination of other resources or production factors required to accomplish the projects, such as materials and tools: "In the factory, men, machines, and materials form bundles by which components are connected and disconnected. In the office, similar bundles connect and disconnect information and channel messages" (Hägerstrand 1970: 149).

This means that time geography is not only a framework that allows us to analyse how and why individuals move. If one reads Hägerstrand in detail, time geography becomes rather more productionist. Time geography is about people, but it is not as much about people as one might think.

Constraints and prism

Constraints, both those given by nature and those that are man-made, affect how individuals can move in time-space. The constraints set the limits for people and things to form bundles in order to accomplish specific projects. The constraints are not only physical (e.g. how transportation technologies place limits on how and where individuals can move) but are also institutional and connected to who has power over space and allows movements of individuals in time-space to take place.

More specifically, the paths of individuals are conditioned by three different sets of time-space constraints that affect the ability to reach and remain at particular locations at specific times (Hägerstrand 1970; Pred 1977).

The first set of constraints are capability constraints, imposed on individuals because of their basic human needs, such as sleep, and tools, such as the means of transportation.

Capability constraints constitute the basic factors limiting the (daily) prism of a person. The prism defines the potential range of a person in time-space, given a specific outset or point of departure. Figure 3.2 illustrates this range for our individual who, say, has to rely on public transportation, goes to work, visits the chess club (pub) and then returns home in the evening. The individual could have travelled further away (she does not take advantage of the entire prism during this average day), but that would have limited the time she was able to stay at a particular place to accomplish particular projects (finish the work tasks, finish the chess game or having a last pint). Also, only by keeping within the prism will a person be able to return to the starting place in time.

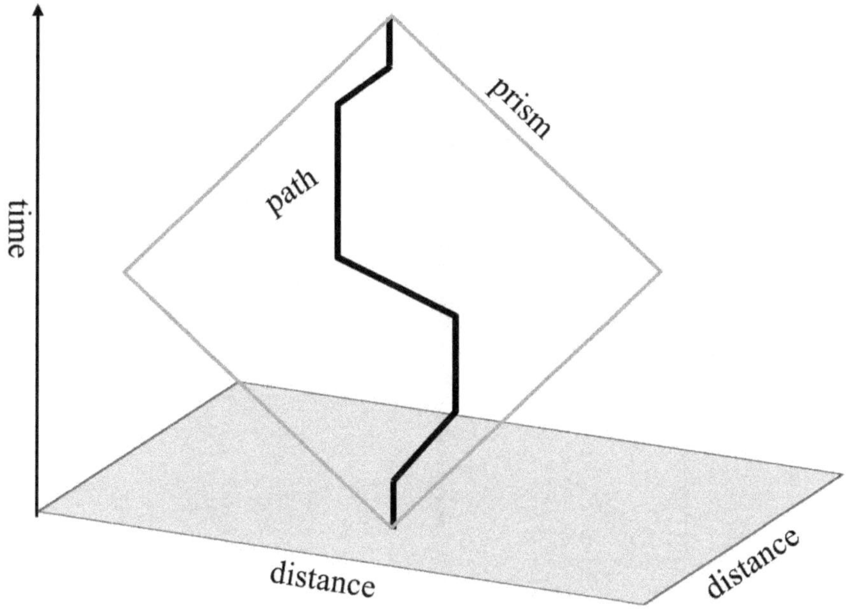

Figure 3.2 The prism
Source: author's drawing based on Hägerstrand (1970: 148).

Restrictions on forming bundles also limit the individual's movements in time-space because all bundles come with minimum limits regarding how long they must be formed in order to achieve the aim of the project (the time needed to finish the work tasks, finish the chess game or drink the pint while covering the necessary items of conversation with the friends at the pub).

Coupling constraints are defined by the requirements on this bundle duration, that is, for how long individuals (and materials or tools) need to meet in order to accomplish specific projects; for example, how long they must come together in a bundle to manufacture a specific product.

The coupling constraints will affect the maximum daily prisms of the individuals that, in Figure 3.3, need to form a bundle with a machine to accomplish a specific production project. Since we return to the example of car production, let us imagine that a bundle needs to be formed to produce a car component. Realizing the project requires two individuals and one machine to coordinate their presence in a bundle in time-space (within the rings) for a certain time (coupling constraints).

The coupling constraints open up alternative uses of time geography. Participating in one bundle in time-space limits the extent to which an individual, a tool or machinery can participate in other bundles. With technological

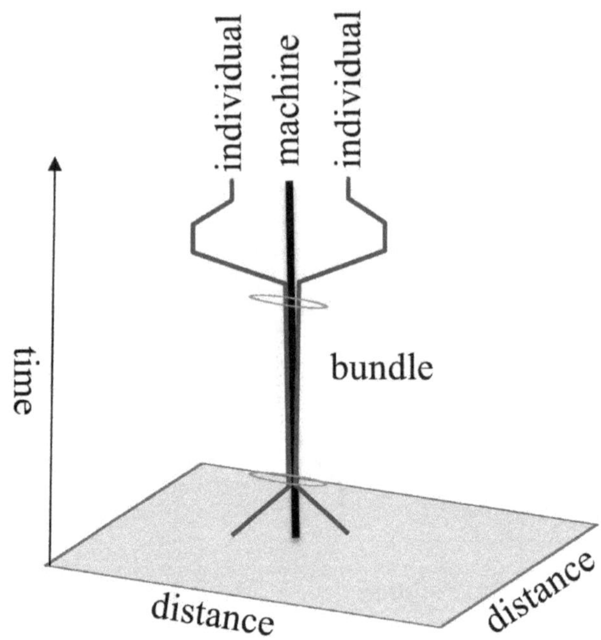

Figure 3.3 A production bundle in time-space between two individuals and a machine
Note: the required length of the bundle imposes coupling constraints.
Source: based on Hägerstrand (1970: 149).

change, for instance a more efficient machine, coupling constraints will decrease, as the same project will only require the formation of a shorter bundle. This enables higher economies of scale or scope. We return to these ideas later in the book.

A last category of constraints, authority constraints, limit how individuals (as well as materials and tools) move in time-space. In all societies, power over which spaces are accessible at certain points in time are controlled and limited by many actors. Authority constraints are those laws and power relations that affect and often decide accessibility in time and space, and restrict how individuals are allowed to move or are conventionally accepted to move.

We can call the areas in time-space that are subject to authority constraints "domains", where entry for participating in projects can be limited: "In time-space, domains appear as cylinders, the insides of which are either not accessible at all or are accessible only upon invitation or after some kind of payment, ceremony, or fight" (Hägerstrand 1970: 150). In Figure 3.4, a prospective entrepreneur is limited from taking part in a productive bundle because of time-space authority constraint: the firm that controls the bundle does not let her

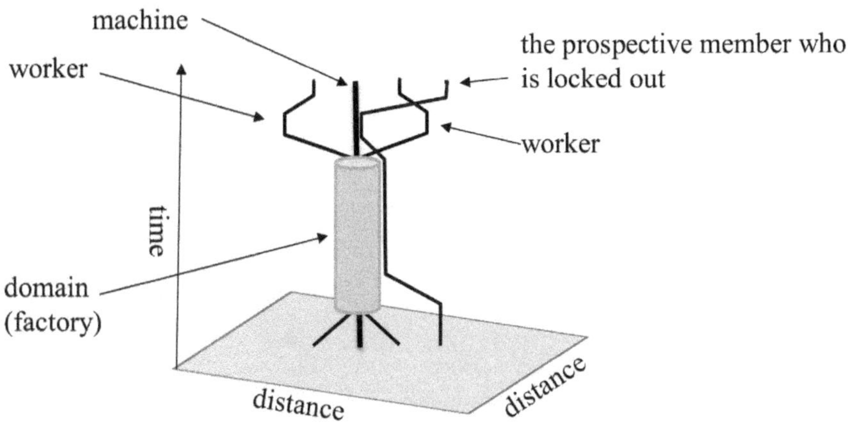

Figure 3.4 A production bundle in time-space between two individuals and a machine, where one prospective bundle member is kept out of the domain because of authority constraints

access the factory premises until after the bundle has been dissolved. It is not a free-for-all to take part in a productive bundle.

Later in this book, we return to the ideas and concepts of time geography. As a next step, however, we need to look at how evolutionary economic geography thinks that production actually takes place. In other words, we need to establish an evolutionary perspective of economic production.

Discussion points

1. Draw a time-space diagram of your overall movements yesterday. Use time geography concepts to describe your path and the projects you participated in.
2. On average, how have time geography constraints changed since the 1970s? Why have they changed?
3. Does time geography make sense in a digital world? Why/why not? (Focus on bundles: are they necessary to produce, consume or transact?)

4

An evolutionary perspective on economic production

> In order to produce efficiently, industries draw on a wide variety of local resources, ranging from professional services to infrastructure and institutions.
>
> F. Neffke, M. Henning & R. Boschma, "How do regions diversify over time?", 51.

What is produced?

Recent research in complexity economics teaches us that what is produced in countries links closely to wealth in those countries but also to the future of growth (Hidalgo *et al.* 2007; Hidalgo & Hausmann 2009). This thinking has not been without consequences for adjacent disciplines. During the last few years, evolutionary economic geographers have been clearly inspired in thinking along such "qualitative" lines in their work around regional economic change and growth (Hidalgo *et al.* 2018). What a region is able to produce tells us a lot about the resources that regions are able to draw on in order to produce a specific thing, how advanced these resources are and how successful that makes the regional economy.

From Chapters 1–3, we already know that regions tend to specialize in producing certain goods and services, and that they need to adjust this sooner or later in order to keep up with developments (selection). Classic accounts in economic geography have done well in terms of identifying regional specialization patterns but not quite as well at explaining their development from an evolutionary point of view.

In order to think more precisely about this, a general framework around regional specialization and economic change – an evolutionary perspective to regional economic production – is required. Some would call it an evolutionary regional "ontology". We are looking for a framework that constructs a view of looking at the world; in this case, how production in regions actually happens, whom it involves and how it changes.

With inspiration from complexity economics on the one hand (Hidalgo *et al.* 2007; Hidalgo & Hausmann 2009), and the resource-based view in management on the other (Penrose 1959; Barney 1991), geographers have recently tried to refine theories to explain better the exact logics of regional economic change (Lawson 1999; Maskell & Malmberg 1999b; Boschma 2004; Neffke *et al.* 2018). This chapter draws on these advancements and aims to develop them further in order to achieve a comprehensive evolutionary perspective on production: a meaningful theoretical way to describe how economic production takes place in regions, and how it changes over time.

Cars

Let us start with a product, one that is important to Gothenburg: a car. Today's cars are complex products, and through a long sequence of developments over time, the economy of Gothenburg has developed the ability to produce cars. Or rather, a renowned firm in Gothenburg has developed the ability to produce some of its components and coordinate the production of the rest, as well as the assembly of the car. In addition, the Gothenburg firm has acquired the ability to market the car once it has been produced and to sell cars all over the world.

What does it take to produce a car in Gothenburg? Obviously, a whole range of things and people, and possibly appropriate regional institutions too. But what is the "best", yet simplest, way to understand how cars are made in Gothenburg and how it continues to change over time?

Let us try a route that goes a bit deeper than traditional economic geography in trying to understand why a firm in Gothenburg has developed a car-making capability that firms in few regions in the world actually have. This route needs geography and time (which is not surprising given the arguments of Chapter 1), resources, firms and people too.

Obviously, all economic approaches involve a great deal of simplification. Defining which objects and which relations between them are the most important is, at the end of the day, a question of perspective and judgement and depends on what you need to explain. It would therefore be unwise to claim that our evolutionary perspective is superior to the ones underpinning traditional economic geography and neoclassical economics. However, in understanding the role of space and time in affecting how production processes happen, there are some advantages speaking in favour of our evolutionary perspective.

The car-making process of interest here is based on the existence of a couple of key resources on-site in Gothenburg: specialized labour, fixed capital in the form of machinery in the Gothenburg factories, materials, suitable infrastructure, automobile-related research groups and a wide range of regional policies targeted at supporting the automobile industry and its development. In Figure 4.1, which summarizes the perspective on car making, these resources are listed at level 1. This list of resources is of course not exhaustive. They are reasonable examples to prove a theoretical point.

Making cars, or any product, requires continuous decisions to put labour, machinery and other things to work. It also requires coordination. Advanced manufacturing work cannot be undertaken randomly. Firms decide and organize production (level 2). For one reason or another (some of which have very historical roots), the firm in Gothenburg decides to use all these resources in Gothenburg to make cars.

It is important to keep in mind that a firm not only decides whether and which resources to use (levels 1 and 2) but also for what end. A different choice can always be made to use the machines, labour and other assets to produce other things. A good example is what could happen when normal market

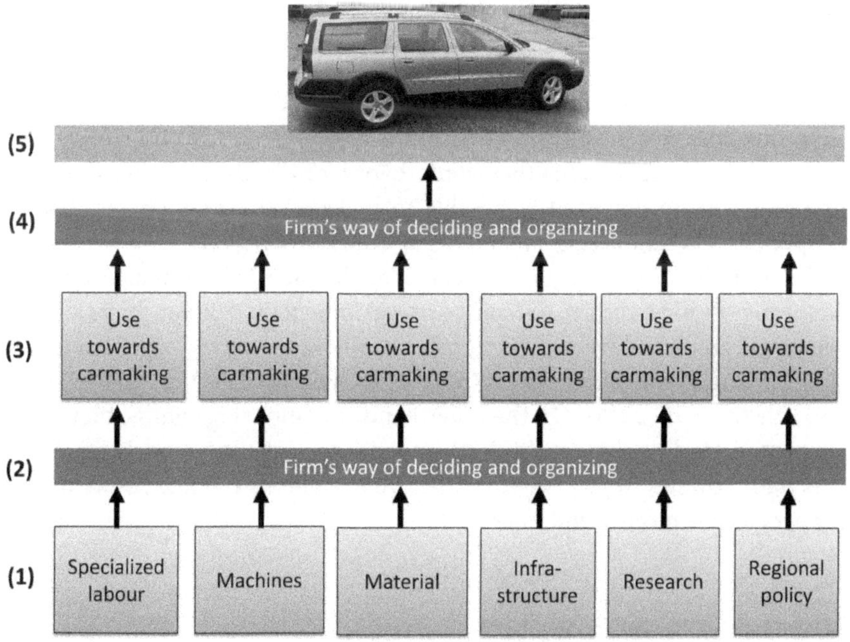

Figure 4.1 How to reach the ability to make a car (slightly simplified)

forces are stalled. During the Covid-19 pandemic, some Swedish manufacturing firms decided to temporarily use their labour, machinery and factories to produce healthcare equipment rather than making their normal products. These decisions were not purely market-driven but show how different production choices can always be made with the particular resources that firms command and coordinate. Often there is a reason why these alternative productions are not selected: they might not be as productive and therefore not as lucrative for firms.

In our case, the firm (or rather, the owners of the firm) in Gothenburg decides to produce cars and organize the production in a certain way that it finds appropriate. This means that it uses the human capital, machinery and other resources towards a certain end (level 3). The specialized labour and other resources are put to work and contribute to car making (and consequently not to producing healthcare equipment or other products).

Let us assume that the firm's way of organizing comes into the picture once more to manage the factory and the tasks that need to be performed there (level 4). Apart from that, a structure is now set up in Gothenburg which actually enables the region, or rather a firm in the region, to make cars (level 5).

With apologies to engineers and car aficionados, the car-making model reduces many complex processes and also abstracts from the huge international trade of semi-finished components that is an integral part of globalization. A quick look at car production makes one thing strikingly obvious: just because a region registers the production of a product (as Gothenburg with cars), this does not mean that firms can derive all the resources needed to make a car in that region. In other words, in order to "make" a car in a modern economy, you do not need to be able to make all the components. Many components and knowledge are imported from other regions.

We bring input imports and exports into the picture later, but so far our perspective imitates the general spirit of development models that many evolutionary geographers have drawn on during recent years: the region (or country) as containing a production system (Maskell & Malmberg 1999b; Hidalgo *et al.* 2007; Neffke *et al.* 2018). On the other hand, traditional economic views on production tend to skip levels (2–4) in order to make the models formally workable. However, we will discover that we need levels 2–4 later, as we make our perspective more evolutionary.

Resources, uses and capabilities

It is time to move from the car to a more general view where we put abstract (theoretical) names on the different levels of the perspective (Figure 4.2).

The idea is exactly the same as with the car example: how different economic levels lead towards accomplishing a good or service. This is also close to a regional application of the so-called resource-based view of the firm. Some of the most important distinctions here, such as the one between resources and the actual use derived from them, were made by the legendary scholar Edith Penrose for the level of the firm (Penrose 1959; Neffke *et al.* 2018). Penrose, and many followers, employ the term "service" of a resource, which is roughly equivalent to the specific "uses" that a resource allows. In order to avoid confusion between theoretical "services" as drawn out of resources, and "services" of the real economy, this book will translate "service" in Penrosian terms to "use".

If we call level 1 (the specialized labour, the machines, etc.) regional resources, all production is based on the use of these resources (otherwise it is not actually production). Resources are defined very broadly as anything that provides the means on which organizations draw in order to achieve a productive capability. Note that we did not say anything about manufacturing versus services (yet). In our perspective, a "product" can be a manufactured physical product, a service or even a combination of the two.

The variations in the terminology used in the literature about (regional) resources are endless. Our resources could also be termed "assets" or "production factors". However, our particular discussion requires conceptual precision. Soon we discuss regional resources more specifically, but for now we stay with a very general idea of resources.

In the first instance, the easiest way to think about resources is to think of a jigsaw puzzle. The completed puzzle is the product, but the individual pieces are not the resources, the wood is. It is easy to get trapped into thinking only about material resources: natural resources are the most obvious ones. But in order to produce something, immaterial resources are often necessary and directly useful, such as skills, technological knowledge or even a particularly ingenious way of organizing work. To accomplish the jigsaw, you also need to understand how and why the resource pieces of the jigsaw can be fitted together in the end.

Developing and sustaining a capability to produce something (level 5, the end goal at the top of the perspective) requires that an organization, often a firm, makes use of the resources (level 2). To take such decisions and organize work, firms draw on their organizational (firm) routines (see Chapter 2). In classic evolutionary work, the study of these firm routines is important. Routines differ between firms, and how firm-specific routines form the competitive basis of firms (and allows them to get ahead in selection processes) has been a core interest of evolutionary micro-economists for a long time (Nelson & Winter 1982).

Nevertheless, as we have learned before, firm routines are not a prime focus for our regional investigations, although organizational routines were an important concept in the early contributions to evolutionary economic geography (Boschma & Frenken 2006). In our perspective, firm routines take a secondary role, although we return to the question of whether there are certain kinds of regional environments that promote good routines to spread in Chapter 8.

As in the resource-based view of the firm, a resource is distinct from the particular uses that are derived from it (Figure 4.2, level 3) (Penrose 1959). The specific uses are represented by the pieces in the jigsaw puzzle: this particular use that the wood (resource) allows for. In the car example, the car producer decided to use the resources and derive specific uses from them in order to achieve the capability to produce a car. For example, the car producer allows parts of the specialized labour (the resource) to be dedicated to assembly work (the use). It employs tools and machinery to deliver uses dedicated to the making of cars. Again, the firm could have chosen to derive uses that produced healthcare equipment or metal boxes instead. The particular use selected is therefore one among competing alternative uses.

Deriving uses from a resource means that the resource is put to work in the production of something and in a certain way, or maybe better in the words of Jane Jacobs (to whom we return many times), in a particular division of labour.

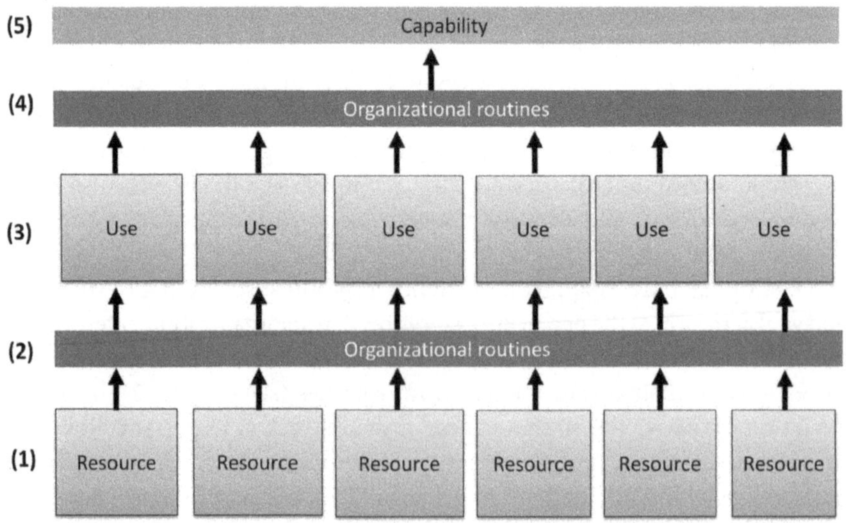

Figure 4.2 Our evolutionary perspective of resources, routines, uses and capabilities

However, deriving the individual uses from the resources does not constitute the ability to make a product. By means of organizational routines, uses have to be orchestrated into bundles to finally achieve capabilities (levels 4 and 5). The opportunity costs – the costs of selecting out alternatives – that firms face when organizing uses of the resources encourage firms to come up with the most productive divisions of labour to reach the end goal: the capability to produce something.

A regional capability essentially marks the ability to produce something in a region. The capability is composed by combining the uses into a bundle, again, by means of the organizational routines. Exactly how resources are combined and turned into capabilities and in what form is decided by the characteristics of resources and uses, and also by the internal routines that the firms possess to combine the resources.

As mentioned earlier, this evolutionary perspective of production is by no means the only economic theory that reasons in a broadly similar way. In some theories about world trade and national specialization, the resources are seen as latent (unobserved) but as producing distinct national specialization patterns. From that point of view, an important obstacle preventing countries from moving into more advanced exports is that they simply do not possess the resources required, nor can they easily build them because they do not have similar resources (Hidalgo *et al.* 2007; Hidalgo & Hausmann 2009). This way of reasoning is very similar to, and actually predates, our evolutionary perspective. However, important aspects need to be added to understand economic change in our time, especially regarding globalization of production, outsourcing and imports of the use of resources. But those will have to wait until we have explored the properties of regional resources further.

Objections and overall lessons

In all, there is much more to be said about the evolutionary perspective from a geographical point of view. For example, what actually makes resources "regional" or more or less localized, and under what conditions can the use of resources be traded? We return to this later in more depth, but let us first sum up some main points around our evolutionary perspective.

First, it is the "stratification" (resources–uses–capabilities) that will result in the perspective becoming an evolutionary one of the regional economy. It will allow us to develop a particular time-dependent view of diversification. So far, however, the sketched perspective is actually not that evolutionary at all.

Second, there are some important issues around resources and the use of resources that we need to sort out to make the evolutionary perspective more geographical. Again, so far there is actually not much space, place or time in it.

Third, the small point made about input (component) import and export is more important than it might seem and is actually pervasive. In the globalized economy, the use derived from resources in only one region is rarely sufficient for a region to develop any capability let alone more advanced capability. Cars, aeroplanes, computers, food and agricultural products, smartphones, ventilation systems and medicines all require sophisticated networks of regional imports and exports. Increasingly, this development is also affecting services, for example knowledge-intensive business services.

Fourth, we have already seen how difficult it is to separate regional capabilities (at regional level) from capabilities in regions (at firm level). Many micro-oriented economic scientists will, with some authority, object to our view: regions do not develop productive capabilities, firms do.

From a purely firm-based point of view (looking at the firm routines), this is true. From our stratified perspective, it is much less true. Firms do develop capabilities, but normally they do this using resources that are both internal to the firm and truly regional. Also, firms can be replaced, and other firms may achieve a regional capability, maybe using even better firm routines. In sum, firms share regional environments, and regional resources condition their development. Therefore, we will continue talking about "regional capabilities", which is the same as "capabilities created and situated in a region". But in one aspect, the critics are completely right: there is a need to specify some more details about (regional) resources.

Discussion points

1. Using the web to explore our evolutionary perspective in the case of a product that is central to your region, what are the important and necessary resources required for its production? What uses of the resources are the most important? Where are the capabilities achieved?
2. What is a firm routine? Can a firm go out of business because of inadequate firm routines?
3. Traditional theories focus mainly on manufacturing goods. Can the evolutionary perspective be used effectively to understand how, for example, knowledge-intensive business services are produced and organized (in regions)?

5

Resources in firms and in regions

> [R]egions grow for similar reasons that firms do: regions host resources, which yield capabilities that expand with their use, that are valuable, rare, specific to economic activities, and hard to access from outside the region.
>
> F. Neffke, M. Hartog, R. Boschma & M. Henning, "Agents of structural change", 27

What resources are

In our evolutionary perspective, resources are something very fundamental. They form the basis on which regional economic change and growth are built. "Resources" also refers to a variety of different things. In this chapter, we explore some of these differences and what they mean for regional economic change.

Working with the idea of resources raises a couple of issues. It is, for instance, hard to find real examples in the business strategy literature of what resources actually are. In Chapter 4, we suggested the following definition: *resources can be anything that provides the means on which organizations draw in order to achieve a capability.* When trying to put this definition of resources to real use, the following problems become apparent:

- *Aggregation*: at what level of aggregation should a resource be defined? For example, is human capital in general a resource, or is a resource more precisely the specializations that the individuals of the labour force possess?
- *Level*: at what level should a resource be defined? Is a university a resource, or are the skilled engineers and the scientific knowledge it produces the resource?

The answer here is pragmatic: it depends on what aggregation and which level the resource is used in order to achieve a capability. If a specialized skill is required to develop a particular capability, that skill is the resource. If skilled engineers in general are required, they are the resource. If the university produces knowledge that is directly put into productive use, the knowledge becomes the resource.

This way of looking at resources provides considerable flexibility and at least some degree of theoretical rigour. This definition of resources is also productionist, in the sense that we are only concerned with resources that can be used in economic production.

With this in mind, frequent examples of resource categories are: natural resources; climate; fixed capital (such as machines); financial capital; the labour force, and the particular skills of the labour force (human capital); infrastructure; proximity to and interaction with other firms (agglomeration); proximity to research organizations and other creators of scientific knowledge; informal institutions; and policy and formal institutions (Porter 1990: ch. 3; Maskell & Malmberg 1999b; Neffke *et al.* 2018).

These different resources, or aspects of them, provide the means on which organizations can draw to achieve a capability. The resources themselves do not enter production but the means that they provide, in the shape of the uses derived from them, are bundled together to develop a capability. A firm, such as the carmaker in Gothenburg, decides to derive a specific use (skilled work) from the labour force in order to produce cars.

It is obvious that not all resources are needed for all kinds of production. A selective choice is involved. Therefore, it does not make a lot of sense to talk about the most important resources in general in the economy, as it varies with industries and also from time to time.

Some resources in the list are intuitive. These are often the material ones: natural resources such as iron ore, gold or fertile soils, or a sunny climate, for instance. These kinds of natural resources have been used to explain regional and country specializations since the earliest theories of trade and economic geography. Natural mineral deposits explain the growth of the mining towns in the middle and north of Sweden, and the demise of some of these towns when their capabilities were selected out of the world market because of competition from other regions. The fertile soils of Scania in the south of Sweden are instrumental to its specialization in agriculture and food production. However, natural occurrence is not sufficient to explain how the resources become regional specialization; someone has to decide to derive appropriate uses from the resources.

Fixed capital are the machines and buildings used for production, and are intuitive "material" resources too. In manufacturing, machines are really important to production (to derive a capability). Financial resources (capital) are needed to establish and run production in most industries. But again, resources need to be put into work. Someone has to decide how to derive the appropriate uses from the resources and refine a particular use for them.

The labour force and its skill set is an extremely important resource in our globalized and technologically sophisticated economy. In the literature, the idea of a local "skill base" has been around for a long time. At the end of the nineteenth century, Alfred Marshall (1890) emphasized the importance of a qualified labour force to regional development. The importance of labour skills as a resource for regional development might be greater today than previously, but it is not new.

Note that technical skills are not the only important skills, because achieving a capability is also about coordination and organization. With complex products, such as a car, coordination plays a huge role: the organizational skills required to run an advanced car factory are complex and essential. In many industries, coordination skills are important resources for firms.

Infrastructure of different kinds, such as airports, harbours and broadband, make up resources in a globalized economy too. The port of Gothenburg is Scandinavia's busiest, even though it is certainly not one of the biggest by global standards. It delivers services for many firms across Scandinavia that allow them to participate in the global exchange of goods and to specialize.

Overall, it is clear how these things and experiences – natural resources, machines, people and their skills as well as physical infrastructure – are resources that can be used to achieve a particular capability in a region, such as producing a car.

By contrast, the importance of more intangible and non-material resources are more difficult to assess. To start with the least difficult ones among these, active research organizations, such as university departments or research institutes, produce knowledge that is important for many industries in developing their production capabilities. For example, in Gothenburg, Chalmers University of Technology carries out research in a wide range of fields, including energy, information and communication science, nano science and transport, involving both industry partners and other research institutes. The range and richness of specialized skills displayed in the research repertoire of this type of leading technology institutes is immense.

In Chapter 3, we briefly discussed (regional) institutions. In the evolutionary framework, informal institutions, such as trust and entrepreneurial traditions, are resources too. Many researchers agree that informal institutions are important to how economies work, but they are also difficult to research. Nevertheless, there are examples: in a radio interview, one of Borås' great textile entrepreneurs told listeners about the entrepreneurial spirit, including both collaboration and competition, that characterized the region during its textile heyday. This is a clear example of how young, closely interacting entrepreneurs can develop institutions such as labour norms and ways of behaving, which influence their businesses, and the development of the region too. (This elaborate description of the regional business climate in the 1940s in Borås by the founder of the leading post order firm ELLOS, Olle Blomquist, in the radio programme STIL broadcast on Swedish National Radio, 29 August 2008.)

This list of resources above is, of course, not exhaustive. Depending on one's concerns, many relevant resources could be added at different levels. In addition, with technological and cognitive change, new resources that were not available or even not relevant to earlier generations are constantly developed and used (Neffke & Henning 2013; Martynovich & Henning 2018). The opposite is also true. Because a resource is on the list does not mean that it is always important in all regions or at all times. The point is that our perspective is open enough for an evolutionary theory to develop and to take change into consideration. The resources that are relevant for economic production tend to change over time.

Finally, regional policy can be a resource that helps to achieve a capability. Policy plays an important role when it comes to establishing formal institutions.

There are a couple of important characteristics that distinguish categories of resources from each other and enable them to assume different roles in processes of regional economic change. Resources matter for production, but their features and roles in economic change are certainly not all the same. First, resources differ because of their "portability": the degree to which resources can be shared or traded across regions. Second, ownership and control aspects determine which resources are regional (available to all firms in a region) or firm-specific, such that they cannot be accessed by other firms. This dimension is referred to as "resource appropriability". Third, resources differ in terms of their "specificity": some resources only have very specific uses, whereas others can serve many different uses (Teece 1982; Porter 1990; Neffke & Henning 2013).

Resources and geography: resource portability

As inferred the previous section, most resources are linked to space. Economic activities take place in particular localities for a reason. One of these reasons is access to resources. Just from looking at a map or thinking about geography, it is apparent that the resource endowment, or resource repertoire, varies across different locations. Different regions offer very different resources. Some locations have an abundance of certain resources while they are completely absent elsewhere. In the earliest eras of economic geography that focused around empirical description, mapping the presence of resources in different places was a key disciplinary objective.

However, looking more closely and more conceptually at this issue, one finds that resources link to space to different extents. Some resources are completely bound to a place and cannot be easily moved whereas others can. A few resources are found almost everywhere: there is no particular source. Traditional Weberian location theory developed a couple of useful stylized concepts around this (Weber 1909). It says that inputs (resources) are either localized (accessible at a given point on the map) or ubiquitous (accessible everywhere at the same cost).

The fact that a resource is "localized" does not mean that it is unique to one specific place. It could actually be available from several different sites. A good example is iron ore. It is a localized resource, but there is not just one mine on earth. In reality, most resources are localized to some extent (accessible at a given point on the map), but many of them, like iron ore, can also be moved or transported to other regions, although this incurs a cost. A localized resource has a source, and there is a cost to moving it or accessing it from distant locations. Iron ore has therefore one key characteristic that it shares with other localized resources: the cost of accessing it can be assumed to vary across space.

In this sense, we can think of space – geographical distance – as a friction that limits access to localized resources. Regions have different resource repertoires because: (1) most resources are localized (having identifiable geographical sources); and (2) there is a cost to moving most resources or accessing resources from outside their locations.

Geography research has developed a range of theories that try to explain why different kinds of resources are localized or why resources are tied to space. This might be trivial in the case of natural resources, but it is much more difficult to explain for institutions. Why it is so hard to copy informal institutions (e.g. "entrepreneurial spirit") from one place to another?

To revisit the resource categories above, Table 5.1 gives some examples of resources and their overall geographical properties.

Looking at Table 5.1, for most of the resource categories, distance is an important factor affecting firms' terms of access to them. Weberian theory seems to have a point here: for localized resources, geographical distance will act as a friction that affects the cost and convenience of use for firms further away.

Fixed capital, such as machines or shipbuilding cranes or even houses, can often be moved. However, to some extent this conclusion can be questioned too. Especially in the case of advanced capital, such as machinery, portability

Table 5.1 Some resource categories and their geographies

Regional resource category	Geography
Natural resources	Identifiable geographical source at extraction point. Can often be transported, but at a cost
Climate	Accessible only at specific points or areas
Fixed capital	Accessible only a specific points in space. Can often be moved, but at a cost
Financial capital	Can easily be moved, at least in principle
Labour force and the particular skills of the labour force (human capital)	Accessible only a specific points in space. Can be moved, but at great cost (and subject to other institutional and social obstacles) (see Chapter 10)
Infrastructure	Accessible only at specific points in space
Proximity to and interaction with other firms (agglomeration)	Geography research has shown that geographical closeness between firms promotes knowledge sharing, facilitates for complex transactions and makes innovative and productive interaction easier (Asheim 2000; see Chapter 7)
Proximity to research organizations and other creators of scientific knowledge	Research findings and applications can in principle and in many cases be accessed from many places, but research has shown that closeness can promote knowledge sharing, facilitate complex transactions and makes innovation easier, even though there are many complications to these processes in the real world (Smith 2007)
Informal institutions	Some institutions, such as trust and entrepreneurial traditions, seem to be very localized phenomena (Gertler 2018). They cannot be separated from the local context and moved, but they do develop across time in particular and unique geographical settings

of the pure product is sometimes not enough to secure its productive use. You also need to create surrounding resources associated with skills and organizational routines in order to make the best use of the fixed capital. In some cases a good written manual is enough, but for many business applications, trade with or sharing of physical resources requires the development of complementary resources that are not as portable or even possible to codify (Gertler 2004; 2018). This is particularly the case where the institutional context is very different from what the designers of, say, an advanced machine had in mind (Törnqvist 1997).

The movement or sharing of resources created by human interaction (such as institutions) have traditionally been seen as far more cumbersome.

In particular, those regional informal institutions that are built around common understandings and cultures are difficult, if not impossible, to transplant elsewhere.

In terms of people and their skills, different economic models make different assumptions. Empirically, we can observe that humans as a resource can be moved, and people do move. Regional "brain-drain" and "brain-gain" processes have considerable consequences for how regions develop (Richardson 2021). In general, however, there is convincing evidence from lots of research that on average and under normal circumstances, people like to stay where they are (Eriksson, Hane-Weijman & Henning 2018).

However, the regional stability of the workforce as a regional resource cannot be taken for granted either. During the decades around the turn of the nineteenth century, more than a million Swedes left to find a new future, primarily in the United States and Canada. Swedish policy-makers were particularly concerned because emigration was selective: thrifty, young and productive people tended to leave. Many Swedish regions were drained of human capital resource. Some emigrants later returned from the USA to Sweden with greater skills and more financial capital (such as my own great-grandfather), but most of this portable resource was lost for the Swedish regions forever. Today, many less fortunate regions suffer from similar "brain-drain" processes.

In sum, resource portability signals the degree to which resources can be moved across regions. To some extent we have already introduced this issue, but this time be aware: it is easy to conflate "resource portability" with the "portability of the use of the resource". Portability of its use is something important to our evolutionary perspective too, but we return to that in Chapter 9.

Often, because resource portability is generally rather low, geographers assume a simplification of this argument and talk about regional resources. With this term, geographers summarize the entire discussion about how the resource repertoire in regions differ, and that firms within a region may not have exclusive but privileged access to the localized resources of a region. Firms in a region share this privileged access (a related argument of "privileged access" to specific assets with regard to multinational enterprises is made by Dunning 1998; also Cantwell & Mudambi 2011). Resource portability is important because it affects how much competitive edge and uniqueness can be developed regionally from a specific resource, especially in the longer run.

Resource appropriability

Ownership and control, or appropriability, is also an important issue when it comes to how resources are used in regions, partly because it influences access to resources and partly because it affects who pays for the resources and who captures the rents (profits) from them. Because of our interest in change, the first dimension is more significant: how appropriability affects access to resources for different firms in a region.

Normally, in the business literature, it is assumed that firms own, or at least control, the use of "their" resources. In fact, it is one of the most important traditional explanations for why firms can compete based on these resources: they can capture the rents from them.

Following our regional lens, it is not quite so straightforward, as many regional resources are actually shared across firms (such as infrastructure) or become available to firms for a certain contract period (like labour). Firms in a region may have privileged access to the resources available in that region, but the appropriability still influences how and when resources are available to participate in change and deliver new uses to firms.

To understand this argument, let us consider three stylized categories of regional resources that depend on how appropriability affects the roles that resources take in processes of change:

1. Organizational resources: these are resources owned and controlled purely by individual firms, research institutes or other organizations. Access to these resources by other actors (firms), or the price charged for using them, is at the complete discretion of the owning firm. Fixed capital – for example, the machines that firms traditionally own – is a typical example of a pure organizational resource.
2. Hybrid resources: these are resources in temporary ownership and/or control of specific firms but which may leave for other firms, sometimes on their own initiative. By far the most important example in this category is labour. Labour can be temporally controlled by one firm, but it is partially a regional resource in the sense that it may switch jobs to the benefit of other firms after the end of its contract period.
3. General resources: these are accessible to all firms in a region and cannot be organizationally owned or controlled by firms. Public infrastructure is an example.

In Gothenburg, the fixed capital of the firms making cars and car parts are typical examples of organizational resources. Machines and real estate belonging to the firms are also regional resources – they are localized to the regions and may be sold to other firms – but they are resources ultimately controlled by the owners, who decide which uses to derive from them. In normal cases, the rents from deriving uses from this category of resources will also be restricted to the owning firm. The labour force working in these facilities in Gothenburg makes up a regional resource too but a hybrid one. The labour force has committed to work for a contract period for a specific firm, but after that they are free to choose to work for other firms (provided they have not committed to refrain from working for a competitor for a specific time, as in "garden leave").

Ultimately, the labour force is a hybrid regional resource to the firms in Gothenburg because Sweden does not permit slavery, and nor do most other, if not all, countries. Completely free movement of labour is, however, not as natural as we would like it to be from a historical point of view. For example, as late as 1944, some agricultural workers in Sweden (*statare*) were still signing up for interminable one-year employment contracts under circumstances that created almost unavoidable dependency from the worker on the estate where they worked.

The fact that labour is nowadays a hybrid regional resource, and not an organizational one, is great progress for human rights and for processes of economic change too. The reason is that people who move between jobs take their skills with them. Through learning-by-doing and other upgrading processes, other firms will access ever better versions of labour resources through labour mobility. Changing jobs is a great way to learn new things and to spread knowledge to new contexts.

General regional resources are often developed due to government initiatives, such as roads, or through partnerships between public and private interests, as in the case of airports. Exactly how this happens, and to what extent, depends on the economic development model of the country or region. In those normal cases, when there are subsidized fees or no fees at all for using general resources, the rents from deriving uses from this resource category are shared across the firms in the region.

Resource specificity

Resources also differ in their specificity. This means that resources are different when it comes to the number and variety of capabilities to which the uses derived from them can be applied. Or in the words of Jane Jacobs, the range of divisions of labour that the resource can deliver uses to (Jacobs 1969). The specificity of resources is an important evolutionary aspect that has a huge impact on the function of the resource in processes of economic change. In the management literature, this is sometimes discussed in terms of how "fungible" resources are (Teece 1982). Factor specificity as a basis for competitiveness is also discussed by Porter (1990).

The specificity of resources differs on a scale from low (very general) to high (very specific) (Neffke & Henning 2013). Some resources are very general, and the different uses derived from these can be of value in many different applications. Some of the skills of the labour force – reading and doing basic calculations, for example – are applicable in almost any industry or activity and can deliver uses to all of those. In other words, resources with these general characteristics have a low degree of specificity. Human capital and competence theory is not new to this kind of thinking, which often splits human capital into general and specialized skills (for example O*NET n.d.; Bowin 2011). A lower specificity is also an obvious feature of many types of infrastructure resources. Roads and broadband contribute with uses that are of great use to many, maybe all, industries, but to a different extent and in different ways.

On the other hand, some resources are far more specific. Machinery and tools may be designed for specific uses in one or a couple of industries, and the uses that they deliver have limited applications outside a specific production realm or industry. Resources with these general characteristics have a high degree of specificity. In Gothenburg, some skills and machines that are used today in the automobile industry offer uses that have few applications in other industries. They are very specific, which limits the potential use of these resources in other applications and industries.

A word of warning though: it is easy to confuse resource specificity with how specialized a set of skills is. Software skills are advanced and specialized (they require great insights into a field and demand a lot from a human's attention) but they still come with a low specificity (in the sense that they can deliver uses to almost all industries).

A good way to understand the specificity argument is to look at economic change. In several European cities, the dismantling of the shipbuilding industry since the 1970s provides great examples of how resource specificity is concomitant with the role of resources in regional change. When the shipbuilding industry in Gothenburg was dismantled, some of the resources were sufficiently non-specific to be used productively in the growing automobile industry, such as parts of the labour force (Eriksson, Henning & Otto 2016). On the other hand, some of the resources were specific to the shipbuilding industry, and for these it was harder to find new productive regional applications to the uses that they could deliver. Some of the fixed capital that the shipyards used, such as the great cranes that today stand idle, provides testimony to the consequences of the limits of reuse implied by resource specificity.

There is a link between resource specificity and economies of scope. Lower resource specificity provides greater chances to create economies of scope for firms and may become a driving force of diversification. Such arguments can also be made on a regional level: a regional resource with low specificity will provide opportunities for regional actors to draw on external economies of scope. We reconnect with this discussion in Chapter 7.

Finally, from an evolutionary point of view, there is a crucial time dimension to the specificity of resources. With technological and cognitive change, as actors discover new uses that can be derived from regional resources the specificity of resources will also change. From a historical point of view, it is particularly easy to see how the specificity of resources changes over time with technological development. This is especially true for those resources that become central to the historically great shifts in technology. Initially, in the postwar period, having access to computer hardware and software skills was a particularly important resource for large process industries, such as steel and paper, and to the banking and finance sectors (Schön 2010). With time and with technological development, access to these types of resources is now a prerequisite for nearly all kinds of activities. Software development and computer skills have changed from being something for dedicated enthusiasts in a select number of industries to an incredibly valuable low-specificity resource creating value in almost any industry. It is true that the resource itself has changed, but with technological and cognitive change the specificity of the regional resource has changed dramatically too.

There is a contrasting position to this when resource specificity increases. If a technology becomes obsolete or goes out of fashion, its specificity will often increase. Right now, combustion engine technology appears to be entering this phase. As other means of driving motors are invented, combustion technologies and the people that know a lot about them become of interest to an ever-declining number of industries and applications.

At the end of the day, very few regional industries rely only on low-specificity resources to achieve their capabilities (products). And if they do, they are likely to be easily mimicked by other regions. Access to resources with high resource specificity can therefore be a sign of uniqueness. On the other hand, it increases the risk associated with the resource becoming obsolete and old fashioned. It is reminiscent of the delicate balance between virtues of regional specialization and the curse of industry obsolescence that characterizes regional path dependency.

Resource properties in combination

Let us conclude the chapter by summarizing the different aspects of resources. Table 5.2 lists the different resource categories and tries to give an intuitive judgement of the level of the different characteristics.

Figure 5.1 summarizes the resource characteristics. The exact position of a particular resource in the triangle will determine the use of the resource in

Table 5.2 An intuitive judgement of the level of different resource characteristics

Regional resource category	Appropriability	Specificity	Portability
Natural resources	Hybrid	Medium	None or low (highly dependent on type)
Climate	General	Low	None
Fixed capital	Organizational	Depending on type of capital	High
Labour force, its productivity and skills	Hybrid	Depending on type of skill	Medium
Infrastructure	General	Low	Low
Financial capital	Hybrid	Low	High
Closeness to and interaction with other firms (agglomeration)	General	High	None
Research organizations and other creators of scientific knowledge	General	Medium	Low
Informal institutions	General	Low	None
Regional policy and formal institutions	General	Medium	None

regional economic change and long-term regional growth process. How? We return to this in the coming chapters, but we can already formulate some propositions at this point:

- Organizational, hybrid and general resources have different functions in regional change. Keeping resources organizational is a way to ensure that firms can capture rents from them. However, this comes at the risk of limiting their potential use in new bundles.
- Hybrid resources are good examples when it comes to explaining why firms in regions are inevitably intertwined.
- Possession of more specific regional resources can be a blessing if they are unique and rare (Neffke *et al.* 2018, on VRIN resources see Barney 1991) but a curse if they prove to be economically obsolete and uninteresting for firms to use in achieving regional capabilities.
- Higher resource portability will make the import of regional resources easier but comes at the risk of regional resources leaving an area so that regional resource repertoires deteriorate.

Before we explore these propositions further, we need to look at why the resource repertoires of regions are not static but change in significant ways. So

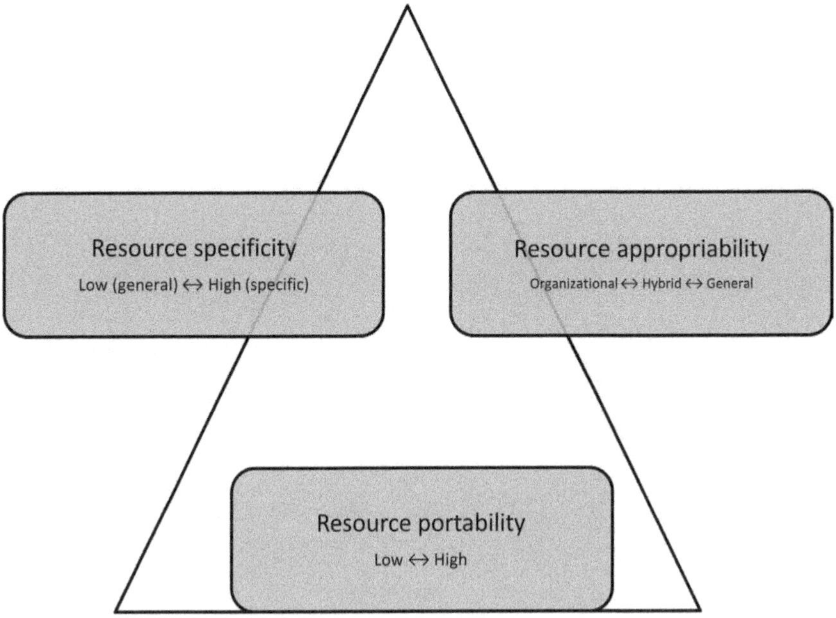

Figure 5.1 The resource characteristics triangle
Note: resource specificity, appropriability and portability conditions determine the use of the resource in regional economic change and long term regional growth processes.

far, we have treated resources in a static way: as if they always exist. In reality, regional resources change all the time, and are in constant need of attention so that they remain available for use. An evolutionary perspective on this is the focus of Chapter 6.

Discussion points

1. How specific should you become when it comes to identifying resources? Is the industry level appropriate, or should you go into the firm level? At some point of aggregation, nearly all resources become unique, of course. What do you think?
2. Can technological change affect how specific regional resources are?
3. In general, have resources become more portable across time? If that is the case, how do you explain regional specializations, clusters and cities?
4. Try to place some of the key resources of your region into the "resource triangle". What does this suggest about the economic vulnerability of your region?

6

Creation, use and curation of regional resources

> Industrial transformation, in brief, means a struggle between new and old, which entails change. Such transformation thus has two sides: the advent of the new and phasing out of the old.
>
> E. Dahmén, "Hur studera industriell utveckling?", 28 (author's translation)

Change in regional resource repertoires

Regional resource repertoires are not static. They change, expand and contract over time. For firms, the resource-based view (Barney 1991) has a lot to say about how resources develop. Inspired by that discussion, in this chapter we investigate how regions create, use and curate their resources.

The right terminology is difficult to find here, because sometimes resources are created in a region (e.g. by a firm) and sometimes they are created by the collective effort of the region. Regions, of course, have no agency by themselves when it comes creating, using and curating resources. However, we follow the standard practice and language of economic geographers when we talk about regional resource creation, use and curation, meaning that resources are created, used and developed by actors, such as firms or public organizations, in a region.

We have already seen how deriving uses from resources requires entrepreneurs and firms to make conscious decisions to do so. The creation and curation of resources require active decisions by regional actors too. Usually, regional resources do not appear out of the blue, and keeping them up to date requires a great deal of effort. Therefore, we will devote special attention to the role that firms and the public sector have in creation and curation. This is an important issue, because previous research in evolutionary economic

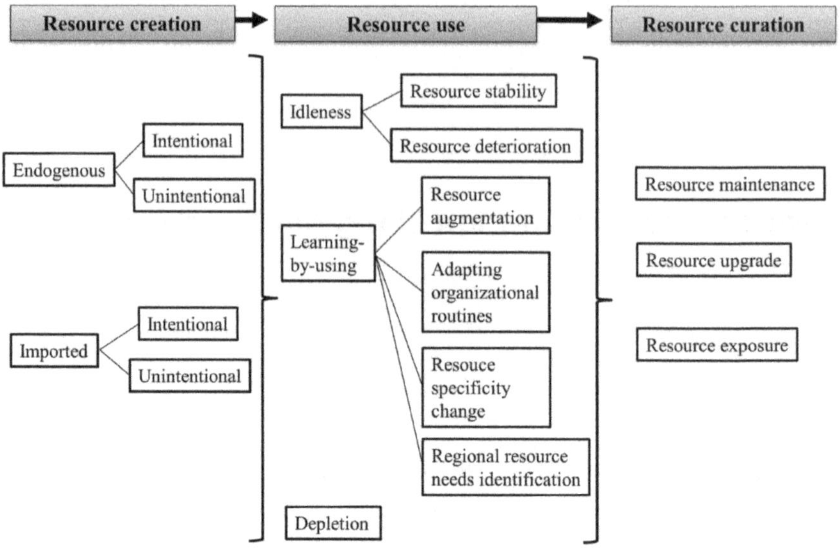

Figure 6.1 Roadmap for the chapter: regional resource creation, use and curation from an evolutionary point of view

geography has been criticized for being imprecise when it comes to who actually promotes path-dependent change in regional economies (Hassink, Isaksen & Trippl 2019). In the following we develop one answer to that question.

Figure 6.1 gives the roadmap for the chapter. First, regional resource creation and its varieties (endogenous and imported) are considered together with the intention involved. Thereafter, we look at the consequences of the use or non-use of regional resources: resource idleness, learning-by-using and resource depletion. We end the chapter by considering resource curation: the ways in which regions have to be looked after and cared for in order to remain as attractive components in bundles that achieve regional capabilities.

Regional resource creation

Regional resource creation processes are some of the most complex processes in market economies, and over time they have grown to become almost endlessly complex. Regional resources are created by millions of decisions taken every day in schools, firms, research agencies and public organizations. These incremental resource-building efforts are the cornerstones of evolutionary economic change. Such processes often go undetected by regional scientists and also by regional theory.

Regional resource creation not only rests on market solutions and the interests of firms. Public and semi-public organizations also have enormously important roles to play in these processes. The importance of the public sector, when it comes to resource creation or co-creation, is ever-increasing in the market economies around the globe, as the economy becomes ever more advanced and resources require even greater investments.

We return to the issue of importing regional resources later in the chapter, but first we explore some of the most important ways in which regional resources are endogenously created in today's regional economies (i.e. created by processes within the region). To start with, Table 6.1 lists some of the measures that are required to create regional resources for our different resource categories. The table also provides some real examples of such measures from Gothenburg and Borås.

The suggestions concerning creation measures behind the regional resources in Table 6.1 have of course been simplified. Each of the aspects in the table has given rise to complete scientific literatures, such as the encompassing literatures about university–firm interaction (Smith 2007) and the one about the properties and mobility of local labour forces (Eriksson, Hane-Weijman & Henning 2018; Eriksson, Lindgren & Malmberg 2008). Nevertheless, Table 6.1 demonstrates an important point: regional resources are created and change over time, usually as the result of active intervention by someone. Again, agency is a required element in the process. The only resources in our list that are not created on the initiative of actors are naturally occurring endowments such as natural resources and climate.

SKF established a fully automated rolling bearing production unit in 2017; Gothenburg Technical Senior High-School was opened in 1998; and Gothenburg Landvetter airport began operating and replaced the old airport in Gothenburg in 1977. These events are all examples of the intentional creation of new regional resources that can deliver new uses to support the capabilities of the region. However, there are degrees to the levels of agency required to create regional resources, and there are limits to the capacities of individual actors to create them.

Other resources are far more difficult to create through initiatives or individual and organizational agency. Regional informal institutions, for example norms and habits such as the entrepreneurial spirit of the textiles cluster in Borås, are very difficult to create intentionally. Indeed, many well-known examples of informal institutions that promote positive economic change and growth – such as the entrepreneurial spirit often associated with industrial districts – have developed collectively over long periods of time. In addition, it is usually very hard to discern how they began. Nevertheless, settings that link people together in a region, such as sport clubs, professional organizations or cultural activities, are vital components in establishing and maintaining informal institutions that also affect regional business.

Table 6.1 Examples of regional resource creation measures

Regional resource category	Examples of creation measures	Gothenburg/Borås example of regional resource creation
Fixed capital (production machinery)	Purchase of fixed capital	SKF establishes a fully automated rolling bearings production unit in 2017
Financial capital	Establishment of local institutions supplying financial capital and venture capital to firms	Volvo Group Venture Capital is founded in 1997 with an office in Gothenburg/Lindholmen
The labour force and its skills	Labour force training: schools, colleges and universities, as well as internal labour force training by firms	Gothenburg Technical Senior High-School is established in 1998 by a collaboration between Volvo Group, Volvo Cars and the Municipality of Gothenburg
Infrastructure (airports, harbours, industrial estates, broadband)	Construction of infrastructure	Gothenburg Landvetter Airport is opened in 1977 and replaces an older airport in the region
Proximity to other firms	Initiatives for establishment of local networks and promoting geographical co-location of firms	The growth of agglomeration of textile firms in Borås in the late 1800s and early 1900s. Establishment and growth of Lindholmen Science Park in Gothenburg, from 2000 onwards
Proximity to research organizations and other creators of scientific knowledge	Establishment of regional universities and research institutes	Establishment of Chalmers University of Technology in Gothenburg, 1829 (by another name)
Informal institutions	Collective efforts that foster common ways of looking at things, such as sports clubs and professional associations	The growth of the entrepreneurial spirit and norms among the entrepreneurs of the Borås textiles cluster
Regional policy	New policy initiatives stimulating the establishment, growth and transformation of local industries	A new framework for regional policy is established by the establishment of Region Västra Götaland (the administrative province where Gothenburg is located) in 1999

Similarly, the geographical concentration of firms, or the agglomeration in which they are located, is a regional resource, because firms can translate proximity into technological learning (more about this in Chapter 8). The co-location of industries happens for economic and social reasons, but agglomeration is difficult to achieve by design. For instance, it is hard to pinpoint an individual who took intentional measures to create a cluster of textile firms in Borås, even though many individual decisions were taken by entrepreneurs, firms and policy-makers that gradually contributed to the growth of that cluster.

There are, however, variations on this. It is far easier to pinpoint when Lindholmen, the science park located at the Gothenburg waterfront that houses a wide range of high-tech firms (including CEVT, Zenseact, Ericsson, Sigma, Valmet and Volvo Group) and educational institutions, was funded and started, even though firms will have taken their own decisions to start or move their activities there.

Given that regional resources are created both intentionally and unintentionally, what or who actually creates them? Table 6.2 shows that regional economic resources are created by many different means and actors, depending on the characteristics of the resource category. For some categories it is easier to say who takes the intentional decision to create them. Local firms are immensely important actors for the creation of regional resources, especially when it comes to fixed and financial capital (organizational resources). It is hard to see, for example, how SKF's establishment of a fully automated rolling bearings production facility in Gothenburg would have come about without the deliberate decisions and actions of SKF.

However, many regional resources that are intentionally created require action by other types of organizations than firms, especially resources that are particularly general. Individual firms have limited incentives to engage in the creation of general regional resources or in many hybrid sources. However, one should not underestimate how many firms engage in their regional contexts and contribute to the development of regional resources that are not necessarily organizational. When firms engage in education initiatives or in technological outreach activities there are certainly aspects of altruism involved too.

Nevertheless, on average and historically, the public sector has played a hugely important role when it comes to taking measures towards regional resource creation, especially when it comes to education and infrastructure. The exact role of the public sector in creating regional resources varies between different countries and modes of economic governance, but it is always important. Moreover, it does not seem that this influence decreases over time; rather, the opposite is the case. In Gothenburg, the public sector (municipality and state) remains the main organizer and funding body for most education initiatives at all levels. The same goes for infrastructural investment. For the enormous Swedish regional

Table 6.2 Main actors that influence regional resource creation

Regional resource category	Main actor influencing their creation ("agency")
Fixed capital (production machinery)	Firms
Financial capital	Firms
Labour force and its skills	Public sector, firms
Infrastructure	Public sector
Proximity to other firms	Firms
Research organizations and other creators of scientific knowledge	Public sector
Informal institutions	Various
Regional policy	Public sector

infrastructural investment scheme Västsvenska paketet (2011–18), which was implemented to improve road, train and public transport infrastructure around Gothenburg, the government is the largest funding body, even though a substantial part is financed through road tolls on users. Regional resource creation is not only about who funds the creation but also about who initiates and coordinates the creation process. Therefore, Table 6.2 attempts to capture the main actor that influences the creation of a resource or is the driving force behind its creation.

An achievement of recent research in geography has been to show how the creation of regional resources requires many different actors to take part in the process, especially when the creation of resources is aimed at delivering economic change (Grillitsch & Sotarauta 2020). Also, as entry barriers to technologies and industries rise in the economy, and as production becomes more complex, stakes in regional resource creation tend to become far higher, at least in some industries and in mature economies. Entry into new, high value-added activities and resource building for them requires vast regional efforts and multi-actor approaches. As an example, Västra Götalandsregionen, the administrative region in which Gothenburg is located, offers a wide range of business support initiatives and co-development opportunities for innovation, competence development, science parks and digitalization. So do many other regional governments in Sweden and elsewhere.

Regionally endogenous resource creation is one thing, but many resources are also portable to varying degrees between regions. This means that not all resources required to achieve a regional capability are necessarily created in that specific region. Studies have shown that when it comes to establishing new directions for regional development, bringing in resources from outside the region (resource import) is often an important factor in explaining how regional change is achieved, especially when imported resources are fruitfully combined with existing ones (Trippl, Grillitsch & Isaksen 2018).

The migration of skilled workers into a region can, for example, create a new resource that benefits regional change. Firms in Gothenburg recruiting specialized IT engineers, for instance from India, or Indian IT firms stationing staff in Gothenburg, are examples of how regional resources are created in Gothenburg by resource import. The import of financial capital is also common and attractive for regions. This activity requires agency. Such initiatives may come from individuals, entrepreneurs or firms (Neffke *et al.* 2018) but are often promoted by other non-firm actors and institutions in regions, such as investment agencies (Trippl, Grillitsch & Isaksen 2018).

In sum, regional resource creation is an uncertain and experimental process. Because of economic fluctuations and rapid technological change, regional resource demands are not easy to predict. The fact that demand and supply of regional resources is seldom in balance is testament to this uncertainty. Also, resource creation has an important time dimension. Whereas some regional resources can be established comparatively quickly (such as infrastructure), others can take years or even decades to create (such as specialized skills or an advanced educational system). Before specific resources have been created, new industries that experience rapid change or expansion sometimes have to use less productive capabilities based on other regional resources that are not optimal (Martynovich & Henning 2018). However, despite the fact that regional resource creation for new industries seems to be very important we actually know relatively little about it.

Only creation of regional resources is normally not enough to make them productive across longer processes of economic change. Over time, most regional resources also need to be used and maintained (curated) to remain attractive components in new regional capabilities.

Regional resource use

What actually happens to a regional resource when it has been created and as it is being used (or not)? It is important to consider this, because a crucial evolutionary argument is that something essential happens as resources are being used, and the evolutionary geographers are not alone in making such arguments.

First, let us look at the alternatives of using and not using a regional resource. With "use", we mean that the regional resources are put to work in order to achieve a regional capability, or in more concrete terms the ability to produce a good or a service in a region, such as a car or a rolling bearing.

Some regional resources, such as natural resources, are completely insensitive to their use: they have been around for thousands of years and remain stable if they are not used. Other resources are not completely insensitive to their use but can be left idle for some time without erosion, such as infrastructure or financial capital.

By contrast, many of the resources that have been identified as being particularly important for long-run competitiveness are sensitive to being left unused (Porter 1990). This is especially the case for human resources, such the skills of the local labour force or regional institutions. Many skills deteriorate quickly when they are not deployed. Consider your own skills: can you recall all the mathematical principles or Latin grammar that you learned in high school? Probably not: lack of use risks them being forgotten.

In addition to this, idle resources that are portable are likely to move to regions where they can find appropriate use. For example, workers might look for opportunities elsewhere. During much of the "record years" period of Swedish economic expansion after the Second World War up to the beginning of the 1970s, the Swedish economy faced a labour shortage. Between 1968 and 1971 more than 100,000 workers left Finland to work in Sweden. This resource import to Swedish regions took place because the Finnish economy was unable to put the resource to appropriate use, and it greatly enriched the resource richness of Swedish regions.

Therefore, resource idleness may result in resource stability (as in the case of the natural resources) or in resource deterioration (as in the case of skills). Because of resource deterioration over time, it becomes more difficult to restart production in a region once the necessary core resources have been left idle for too long.

The second aspect of regional resource use is learning-by-using. The literature on the resource-based view of firms offers an insight into how resources develop with their use: some resources actually improve and become more competitive as they are used (Penrose 1959). More concretely, as resources are put to use by taking advantage of the capabilities derived from them, they grow in their use and change character. Also, in the case of cities, Jane Jacobs regarded economic activities as being processes of discovery and exploration that "suggest" new products and processes (Jacobs 1969). When putting regional resources to work, individuals, firms and organizations find out more about them and what they can be used for.

There are several kinds of learning-by-using. They are distinct and have different evolutionary consequences. Some regional resources themselves change and improve when they are used for achieving a capability. Let us call this process *resource-augmentation through learning-by-using* (Figure 6.1). But let us think about this augmentation, or growth of a resource, in qualitative as well as quantitative terms. Some resources both grow in substance and become better with their use.

An example is worker skills and how people learn through experience. For example, this happens when car industry workers in Gothenburg undertake tasks more quickly and solve problems faster than a new colleague does, just because of their vast working experience in the firm or in the industry. The same happens to institutions. When people rely on (use) regional institutions to achieve capabilities, they also change. Resources based on people and their connections change as they are used, and often they grow and improve by an evolutionary logic.

Another related aspect promoting the efficient use of a regional resource is that regional actors learn how to organize work better. They adapt organizational routines through learning-by-using. This can be difficult to separate from the creation of a resource. When firms buy new machines, as when SKF in Gothenburg invests in a new automated production unit, they need to adapt and refine organizational routines that fit the use of those resources. Over time, as firms organize resources in their bundles, they also learn incrementally how to adapt organizational routines to make the best use of the resources in the bundle and get ahead in selection processes.

The use of resources also involves a learning-by-using process about the specificity of a resource (i.e. how many different types of uses the resource can deliver). The idea behind resource specificity and how it can change over time were discussed in Chapter 5. During the use of a regional resource, a learning process takes place that changes its specificity as new applications are discovered. Essentially this involves opportunities for developing economies of scale. We can term this *resource specificity decrease through learning-by-using.*

Jane Jacobs describes this as one of the main reasons why regions or cities diversify. In her terms, ideas and materials that are used (i.e. resources) in a city "suggest" diversification possibilities. The move that mechanical workshops once made into shipbuilding, for example in Gothenburg, thereby establishing its shipbuilding specialization, at least partly reflects how they discovered that the resources they used (accomplishing a wide range of mechanical products) could be made productive in ship repair and shipbuilding. They, or rather someone, discovered this and expanded the uses from available regional resources in order to attain new capabilities.

Jane Jacobs also discusses a final learning-by-using effect that has far-reaching implications. One of the most famous innovation and entrepreneurship stories in Gothenburg is how the rolling bearing manufacturer SKF was funded, based on a particular innovation by the engineer Sven Wingquist. Wingquist's innovation was a response to production issues in the local textile industry, where the productivity of the machines was compromised because of the rigid design of bearings. His more flexible rolling bearing innovation grew into a business that was to become the Gothenburg-based multinational SKF. In Jacobs' terms, this is a typical example of diversification based on the observed problems of existing economic activities. Basically, by using a resource you learn about other regional resources that you need in order to create and improve. This represents *regional resource-needs identification through learning-by-using*.

Not all stories about resource use involve dynamic learning and roaring evolutionary success. In some cases, resources, especially material ones, are simply worn out with time and consumed. Natural resources might simply run out and are no longer available for regional development. Coal mining or iron ore are obvious examples. Especially in remote locations, there many examples where finite resources lead to complete regional demise. Let us call this *regional resource depletion by use*.

Not all resources last forever. Nevertheless, with "curation" they could be made to last for much longer.

Regional resource curation

Most regional resources risk depletion from overuse: it is not a phenomenon limited to natural resources. For example, both machines and institutions have to be maintained and cared for in order to stay productive. In fact, in modern economies with constant technological and structural change, regional resources have to be constantly maintained and upgraded. Depreciation of capital is allowed for in conventional economic theory. However, from an evolutionary point of view the opposite, resource curation, is equally important and interesting. Keeping regional resources attractive over time and making them attractive candidates for participating in regional change requires much more than simply their creation.

Regional resource curation comprises three steps: (1) maintenance of regional resources; (2) upgrading of regional resources; and (3) making regional resources visible and attractive candidates to include in new bundles.

Regional resource curation can be expensive, and it requires selection by individuals, firms, the public sector and other regional organizations about which resources to maintain, update and expose, and which to drop from the repertoire. Sometimes the selection is actively or intentionally made, involving strategic decision-making. Sometimes it is passive or unintentional, for example due to lack of general interest in maintaining resources in a specific industry.

The maintenance of regional resources involves keeping them productive over time and as close to the way they were created as possible. Table 6.3 lists

Table 6.3 Regional resource curation measures (examples)

Regional resource category	Maintenance measures	Upgrade measures	Exposure measures
Fixed capital (production machinery)	Regular technical maintenance	Technical upgrading	Marketing, trade fairs, seminars, showcasing examples of regional products
Financial capital	Capital inflow	New ways of financing economic activities	Regional capital market days
Labour force and its skills	Closely connected to use of the labour force and its skills and experience creation	Post-education training, update events, lectures, workshops	Employment offices, showcasing regional skill specialties
Infrastructure (airports, harbours, industrial estates, broadband)	Securing safety of use and functionality	Technical upgrading	Information campaigns
Proximity to other firms	Probably most efficiently curated in an indirect way, e.g. through labour force upgrading		Cluster visibility, showcasing regional skill specialties
Research organizations and other creators of scientific knowledge	Ensure funding	Learning and technical upgrading of equipment	Showcasing examples of local collaboration
Informal institutions	Acceptance of and compliance to institutions		
Regional policy	Acceptance of and compliance with regional policy	Learning, constant updating and reformulation	Reach-out campaigns

some of the ways in which regional resources can be maintained across reasonable amounts of time. Physical infrastructure needs to be maintained for it to stay useful to the economic activities in the region. In a modern city, such as Gothenburg, infrastructure maintenance, performed by a wide range of public actors and private firms, is a never-ending task to keep the city's economy running. The machinery used in production is another obvious example of regional resources that need regular maintenance and checks to ensure that they are working properly.

Intangible regional resources require maintenance too. Consider regional institutions such as the entrepreneurial spirit of some regions: here, institutional creation without ongoing maintenance would not be useful. The economic impact of institutions rests on the fact that the regional collective maintains them. Without this input, institutions simply cease to exist.

One of the most discussed curation issues in today's economies concern the development and upgrading of the regional labour force's skill set, and how to adapt them to a rapidly digitalizing economy (World Economic Forum 2016). The debate around the computerization and automation of work has become increasingly intense in recent years, with policy-makers around the world asking what they can do to keep their regional human capital attractive in an economy that uses ever more advanced varieties of machine learning, robots and computers. Because education and training historically has been the safest route to employment, the debate around the skills' resource has focused on regional education and post-education training structures as the most important measures for upgrading human capital. So far, however, because our Western institutional legacy is focused on building skills when people are young rather than curating them as people get older and more experienced, few regions have found good solutions to this problem.

The technological revolution also means that conditions for upgrading those human resources have changed. Updating labour skills has become easier as digitalization has improved information access. However, the maintenance principles for fixed capital change too. Suppliers of fixed capital can monitor the exact status of machinery and equipment through remote sensors and make maintenance more needs-based and efficient.

Regional resources also need to be discovered, and regional actors need to know where to find them. To some extent this is about marketing and creating actor links, for example letting others know what the specialized fixed capital of firms in a region can do or linking financial capital to relevant firms. For labour, employment offices work to match workers and firms. The marketing campaigns that regions and clusters undertake (see also Chapter 8) are examples of curating regional resources, because they show what regional economic specializations use resources for, and also suggest alternative uses. In all, regional resource exposure measures vary between solving incomplete information problems to pure marketing.

Creation, use and curation

At times, it is admittedly hard to distinguish between the curation of existing regional resources and the creation of new ones. This is often a matter of degree. When is a regional resource completely new? New infrastructure is easy to identify and new human capital is often much more difficult to distinguish; this is, again, a matter of degree.

In examining what happens during regional resource creation, use and curation, the question arises as to what this all means for the nature and direction of regional economic change. Evolutionary theory teaches us that through learning-by-using effects and the maintenance and upgrading, regional economies are likely to follow path-dependent ways of change. The use of resources and how curation works tells us a great deal about why regions become so entrenched in their regional specializations. This is the topic of Chapter 7.

Let us end the chapter with a brief example, which reveals a great deal about how regions face new challenges in their creation, use and curation of resources. The car industry is changing rapidly with the introduction of electric motors. According to the CEO of Volvo Cars based in Gothenburg, Håkan Samuelsson, a transition from combustion to electric vehicles requires the recruitment of new engineers and management staff with targeted competences, as well as extraordinary retraining of existing staff. At some point, the transition might even involve making people with less suitable competences redundant (SvD 2019a).

This transition demonstrates an application of evolutionary theory and how economic and technological change link to resource creation and curation. Regional change into the electric car paradigm requires new resources to be created, new uses to be derived from them and some curation of existing resources, whereas some old uses are becoming obsolete. Handling this is a huge challenge for traditional automakers and car-making regions, and requires them to reform their organizational routines. However, just creating new regional resources in times of great change is not usually sufficient, partly because resources are scarce and partly because it often makes sense to reuse some resources. For example, the transition to electric vehicles also requires the curation of regional resources. Ulrika Lindstrand, chairperson of the engineers' labour union in Gothenburg, has pointed to the scope for retraining engineers, something that has already started with a joint initiative between Swedish universities and the labour union called "Study Friday" (SvD 2019b). In sum, this is an example of agency-led resource curation in practice.

Discussion points

1. Is it necessary to curate regional resources? Why?
2. Have you used a "resource" and realized that it could be used for something other than the intended use?

3. Identify some of the core regional resource-creating organizations in your region. Which resources do they create? How? How do they decide which resources to create?
4. Try to identify some historical regional economic resources that were left idle and deteriorated into obsolescence. Why were they left idle? Which resources were created to replace them (if at all)?
5. What role does the public sector play in creating regional resources? Should it also engage in creating resources that are organizational? If so, to what extent?

7

Regional economic change: path dependency and radical transformation

> [N]ew goods and services [...] do not come out of thin air. New work arises upon existing work; it requires "parent" work.
>
> J. Jacobs, *The Economy of Cities*, 55

More evolution!

Because regional economic change is so important for how workers make a living and is fundamental for people's welfare, one of the main goals for an economic science must be to understand how regional economic change works. So far, we have dealt with a very basic evolutionary regional perspective, trying to establish: the most important the actors of a regional economy; how these actors create, use and curate resources to derive uses from them; important aspects of regional resources; and the various way in which firms can combine resource uses to achieve regional capabilities.

However, so far we have not discussed regional economic change itself. It is time to become a bit more evolutionary in our investigation. This chapter looks at different approaches to thinking about regional economic change and how it is likely to happen.

A basic tenet of evolutionary economic geography is that the structure of regional economies condition (but do not determine) the qualitative future of the economies. To put it another way: if we know enough about a regional economy, we can estimate the probability of it changing in a particular direction in the future. In evolutionary economic geography, it is how resources are created, used and curated that provide clues to the future of regional economic change.

Regional economic change happens by degree, lying somewhere between incremental and radical change. This terminology is commonplace in the innovation literature, but it is often used in regional contexts too.

Most of the changes that take place in regional market economies are relatively undramatic and incremental. The introduction of new products or production methods, for example, builds on existing and established use of resources, such as skills and the presence of technologies and institutions (Freeman & Louça 2001; Perez 2010). During such change, established firms have many advantages over new ones. They are already familiar with production processes and the appropriate organizational modes (Tushman & Anderson 1986). In the market economy, such incremental change is part of everyday business.

However, incremental change takes many forms and occurs to different degrees. An example of regional incremental economic change is the development of a new product variety, for example a new variation on an existing car. Such processes are relatively easy to spot at case study level. Most firms that experience competition try to stay ahead of selection pressures by developing their products and processes constantly, little by little.

At the regional level, it is sometimes difficult to assess if economic change is incremental or not. The following is a great example of how complex the process of change can become, in which the links between new and old need to be observed in order to be able to assess how incremental change actually is.

During the Swedish textile crisis in the 1960s and 1970s, when much of the labour-intensive work moved to lower-cost countries, the textile cluster in Borås suffered a great deal. Replacing some of the textile activities, Ericsson, the electronics/telecom firm, opened a plant in Borås in 1970. Some of the skills of the previous textile workers were transferable to the production of electronics, which required precise manual assembly work. The town developed a new capability through its labour resource. A twist to this story is that the Ericsson plant still exists in Borås but now specializes in research and development, testing and coordinating logistics operations. In a stepwise and incremental manner, this part of the regional economy has moved a long way from its textile past.*

The Borås example also poses an important question. In terms of the evolutionary approach, on what level is incremental regional economic change actually happening? Is it happening among the regional resources? In the uses derived from them? Or in the regional capabilities that are achieved?

---

* I would like to thank employees at the Ericsson plant in Borås for sharing this example with me.

Keeping the notion of change at a very general level, we can decide that regional stepwise change could happen at all the levels of our evolutionary perspective. Regional resources can change incrementally as can regional capabilities. Often, these changes at the different levels are connected (but not always), and our evolutionary perspective enables us to explain how incremental changes at the different levels are connected within regions.

In contrast to incremental regional change, radical regional changes are economic leaps that happen when something very different becomes established in a regional economy compared to what was there before. Radical change can happen at all levels of our evolutionary perspective: to the regional resources available, or in the shape of a drastic shift to the production of something completely different.

A good indicator of radical regional change is when previously established resources and uses are not particularly important for an emerging new regional capability. In comparatively stable economies such as Sweden's, it is difficult to find examples of such radical regional economic change. And as shown by the technology management literature, really fundamental radical change, or "disruptions", are not particularly common in other economies either (Tushman & Anderson 1986). Nevertheless, they do happen. The great expansion of knowledge-intensive IT services in the 1990s is close to being such a radical change. In 2010, this global industry offered services that were unheard of in the early 1990s, deriving uses from a vast range of new technologies, hardware and skills. In Sweden, the industry expanded to employ more than 100,000 workers in 2010, a sizeable proportion of employment. This industry required the creation of many new resources, such as the development of technology and training skilled staff. It took time to make specialized resources available to this emerging industry (Martynovich & Henning 2018).

Possibly the most important aspect of regional economic change is how change on one level of the evolutionary perspective (for example in regional resources) can lead to radical change at other levels (for example in capabilities). Given our evolutionary perspective of production and how resources link to capabilities, it would be difficult to achieve radical change on one level without radical change on other levels. Radical change in regional capabilities, for example when Gothenburg gradually became able to deliver advanced IT services to its multinationals on a large scale in the 1990s, requires the creation of new regional resources too.

At times, especially during economic crises and when there are great technological breakthroughs (such as in the IT sector of the 1990s), regional radical change can occur surprisingly quickly. Overall, the observable economic capabilities of Gothenburg have changed incrementally over time. However, the shipyard closures took place during a comparatively compressed period during the 1970s and 1980s. This was regional radical change in one of its most extreme forms.

There is of course something in the distinction between incremental and radical change that has to do with how processes play out across time. Because regional economic change can take place at all the levels of the evolutionary perspective, there are also often time lags between change at the different levels. Regional resources might change whereas the uses derived from them do not (or not as quickly). Alternatively, the uses derived from the resources alter but the resources themselves do not. Such lags are common in regional economies and may result in resource idleness, which risks a deterioration of regional resources.

To some extent, we saw in Chapter 6 what resource idleness can do. In many old industrial regions across Europe (including regions close to Gothenburg) this is exactly what happened with the deindustrialization process after the 1970s. The uses that were derived from the local labour force had to be changed, but the labour force did not keep up. Some previous uses were just not as relevant any more, and the resulting unemployment precipitated a drastic change of fortune for many workers. It is sometimes claimed that these kinds of old industrial regions suffered from economic change during deindustrialization, but the evolutionary perspective tells a different story. In fact, these regions did not change enough. Far more change, or at least complementary change on more levels, would have helped both the deindustrializing regions and the workers. Indeed, change at the different levels of our evolutionary

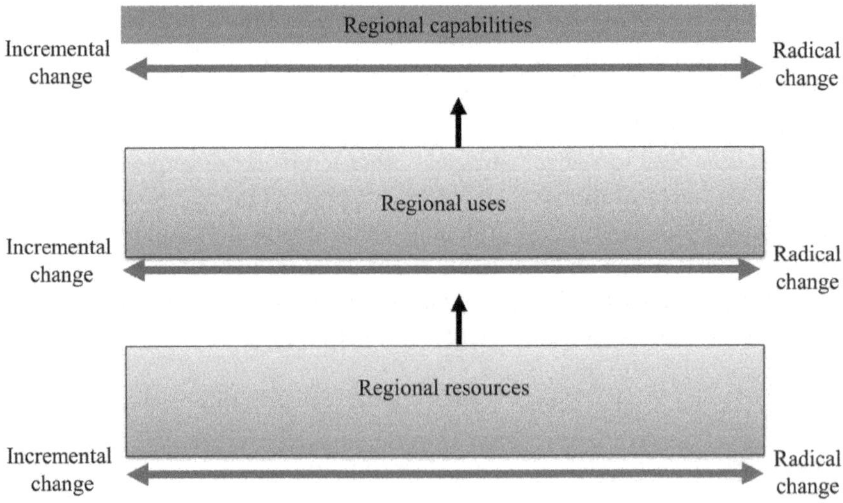

Figure 7.1 Radical and incremental change in regional economies

perspective is sometimes coordinated, but the lags that sometimes occur result in imbalances between the different levels of a regional economy: resources, derived uses and capabilities.

To summarize these ideas about the degree of change in regional economies, between radical change and incremental change, Figure 7.1 depicts change on different levels of the perspective. Finally, it is important to remember that regional economic change is a matter of degree: more or less radical or incremental, rather than always being extreme.

Incremental industrial change and branching processes

There is a long-standing argument in the regional literature that "history matters" to economic change within a region (and especially – of course – to incremental change) (Henning, Stam & Wenting 2013). This makes a lot of sense as a general statement: it is easy to find examples of how history matters in what is observable.

Using our evolutionary perspective, we can become far more precise about how history impacts on regional economic change and what actually matters. A region's history is certainly linked to discussions of incremental change. In this section, we explore how they are connected. In order to do so, we also need to explore the idea of regional economic change as a branching process (Frenken & Boschma 2007) and as a process dominated by related diversification into new activities (Neffke, Henning & Boschma 2011; Fitjar & Timmermans 2017).

Our starting point is necessarily going to fall somewhere within the overall course of a region's economic history: between their beginning and their end as regional economies. There are, however, also (some particular) moments that could be seen as the end and the start of regional history (or at least resurgence), and we do not have to go back too far to find them.

Nevertheless, in practice a pristine economic landscape where regional resources do not exist, and where history does not matter in any way, is hard to find. When did Gothenburg, or any major city, actually start as an economic environment? Because most regional change is incremental and builds on established resources, it is also, in most cases, difficult to imagine a world where new economic activities do not have to take into account their relationship with established regional resource structures. We have to start somewhere in the middle, in theory and in practice.

In Chapter 6, we learned that Jane Jacobs, the journalist who wrote a series of books about cities and evolutionary economics, famously argued that existing production in a city (region) offers important clues to future production, that is, the new regional capabilities that could be developed. She wrote, with an epic formulation, that old work "suggests" new work. She also said that the suggestions could be of two kinds: either made by innovation and learning from what you already have or make (using skills or materials in the production of new things), or by necessity (problem solving) (Jacobs 1969).

Tying these ideas back to the evolutionary perspective, it should be clear that when regional resources deliver uses to achieve a particular regional capability, learning and discovery processes are also going on all the time (Penrose 1959; Neffke & Henning 2013). We have also learned that regional resources are very different in their character, and that their specificity is a key aspect. When specificity is lowered, by technological change, by learning-by-using or by resource curation, the uses derived from resources can be put to work to achieve new regional capabilities.

This is exactly what happens when there is incremental regional change: alternative uses are found for established regional resources. In Borås, some of the former textile workers started to work on the assembly of electronic products. An alternative capability was discovered, which could, at least partly, make new use of an established, regional labour resource.

This kind of incremental regional change is summarized in Figures 7.2 and 7.3, deploying the evolutionary perspective on how production happens. In Figure 7.2, firms in a region use the regional resources to derive a certain set of uses, resulting in bundles of uses that achieve three different regional capabilities, for example bread, textiles and blacksmith products. In Figure 7.3, things have changed. A firm has decided to reallocate the use of regional resources 3 and 4, to derive different uses: 6 and 7 instead. The firm uses this to produce a new regional capability, 4. For example, to produce electronic circuit boards instead of textiles.

Again, empirical evidence points to the fact that regional economic change often happens in this incremental way: using established regional resources to do something new (achieving a different capability) (Hidalgo *et al.* 2018; Content & Frenken 2016). This is a low-friction way of achieving regional economic change.

Most of the time the real processes of regional change are not nearly as neat; Figures 7.2 and 7.3 are just stylized examples to prove a basic empirical point about incremental regional change as resource reuse. In the real world, regional change often involves recombinations and cross-combinations of uses derived from resources with different portability, appropriability and specificities, but also recombinations with imported uses. This is something that we return to in Chapter 10.

It is natural to connect this idea about change to the idea of Schumpeter's, about innovations often being "new combinations". To us, economic change

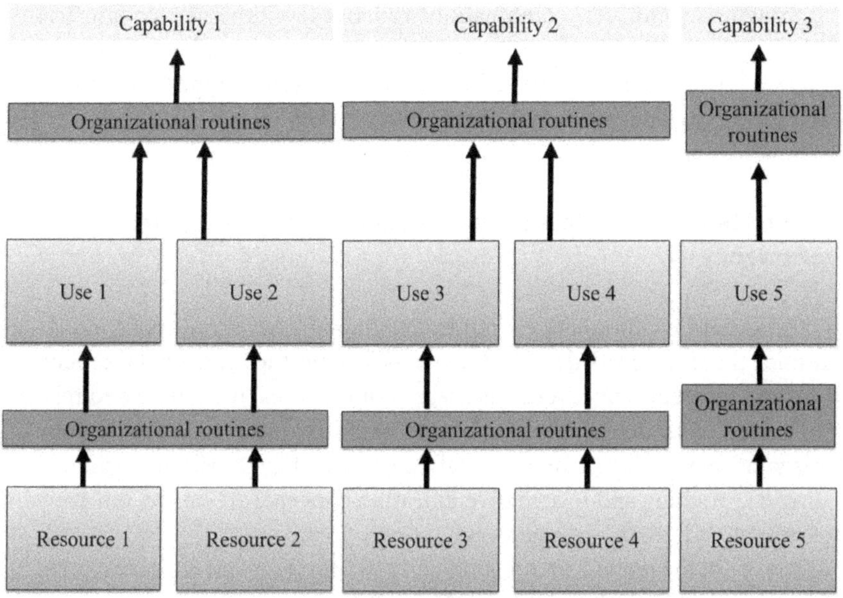

Figure 7.2 Three capabilities achieved in a regional economy

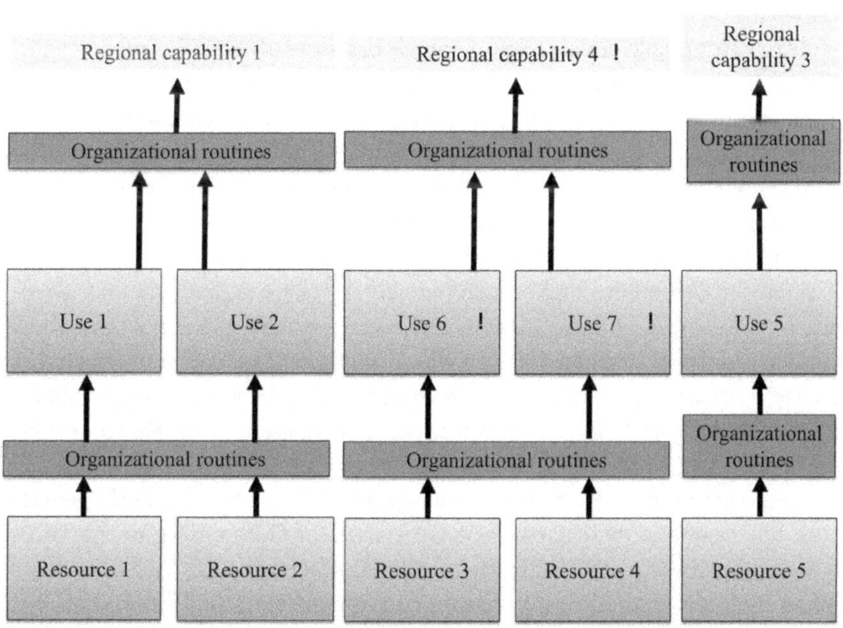

Figure 7.3 Change of uses derived, enabling achievement of regional capability 4

and growth is about new combinations too, but this time new combinations of regionally derived uses rearranged into different bundles whereby new regional capabilities are achieved. In fact, this is the typical type of evolutionary incremental regional economic change in a nutshell.

Regional branching, related diversification and regional path dependency

In recent years, evolutionary economic geographers have made great efforts to put finer theoretical words to and contexts around the incremental processes of structural change, by discussing ideas about regional branching and related diversification in detail. These concepts add a structured understanding to the evolutionary idea of incremental economic change within regions. The regional branching and related diversification concepts are linked, but they do not refer to exactly the same process.

First of all, the metaphor of regional branching (Frenken & Boschma 2007) gives us a picture of how incremental regional economic change takes place; a process in which new productive capabilities follow from old, like the branches of a tree. It is a powerful theoretical analogy but it sometimes becomes imprecise in the details. It is often empirically unclear what the branches actually are and what exactly make them connected in a regional economy.

Our evolutionary perspective of course has a great reply. For many evolutionary economic geographers, the underlying structure making the regional branching possible is the setup of regional resources, their characteristics and the bundling of the uses derived from them. Regional economic branching happens where a new regional capability is developed from a rebundling of uses, employing the same regional resources or regional resources that have been curated to deliver a new set of uses.

What the capabilities that branch out actually share is precisely that: a reliance on the same or updated versions of the same resources. To understand how and when different uses are derived where and when, we can apply the entire repertoire of concepts describing the characteristics of resources (portability, appropriability, specificity) and how they are created, used and curated over time.

On the one hand, regional branching captures processes that link old economic activities (capabilities) to new ones in regions on a fairly general level. For example, the carmaker Volvo started in Gothenburg in the 1920s as a side business to the rolling bearing manufacturer SKF. The firms were linked by interpersonal ties: the first management team had worked at SKF, and SKF provided initial financial support. This is regional branching, because without the presence of SKF in Gothenburg and its financial capital and human resources there would be no Volvo. However, the main links between old and new are based on new uses of rather general resources in this case. Yet, the resources provided branching opportunities for the economy of Gothenburg.

On the other hand, in the case of the textile workers in Borås and the regional branching from the textile branch to the assembly of electronics, the low portability but medium specificity of the labour resource, and the way it had been used to acquire experience in production, contributed to the development of a new regional capability. Different uses were derived from a rather specific established regional resource. Both the Volvo example and the Borås story are examples of regional branching, but on the basis of different regional resources.

This therefore brings us directly to the second idea, which is one of the most fundamental to the principles of evolutionary economic geography: the idea of related diversification in regional economies. From the point of view of our evolutionary perspective, related diversification explains in greater detail why regional branching is more likely to happen as an outcome of the use of technology and learning. It adds further analytical sharpness to the branching metaphor.

Inspired by developments in complexity economics, empirical research in evolutionary economic geography has consistently found that regions are likely to develop new economic activities that are related to the old ones (Neffke, Henning & Boschma 2011; Boschma, Minondo & Navarro 2013; Essletzbichler 2015). Regions diversify into related activities: they branch out into related economic capabilities. This argument links well to the ideas about the different kinds of learning-by-using processes that happen as resources are used in regions. This is very important, but we also know that the specificity of resources can change in ways other than through learning, for example through technological change (Chapter 4).

We are completely focusing on opportunities for regional change. However, it should be noted that this way of thinking is by no means new when it comes to how organizations develop new activities. The ideas about related diversification have a long history in management literature (Neffke & Henning 2013).

Now, the big question is what determines which capabilities are related? The evolutionary perspective offers a straightforward answer: those regional capabilities that partly rely on uses derived from the same regional resources are related. We say "partly", because we want to allow for the Schumpeterian recombination: new capabilities nearly always involve some degree of recombination with new resources. In the 1970s, textiles and the assembly of electronics were (quite surprisingly) related because they relied partly on the same resource (labour). However, in Borås, this was not the only condition for regional branching.

Another slightly unexpected example of related diversification in regional economies is provided by an earlier case. With the advent of steel-hulled ships, it would be reasonable to assume that established shipyards would have a great competitive edge because they already had organized regional uses in the building of wooden ships. But in many cases, related diversification into modern shipbuilding took a very different path. In Gothenburg, for example, the great shipyard Götaverken started out as a mechanics and metal workshop and not as a shipyard. The mechanics and metal business was more related to modern shipyards than old-style ship building. The steel-fabricated vessels required a set of resource uses that firms in the mechanics and metal business could achieve more skilfully. However, the workshops did not turn straight to ship building. The process took time, with experience gathered from manufacturing and in sequential moves towards ever more advanced products before the workshops arrived at making ships. Incremental change was achieved by resource creation, curation and related diversification.

In sum, recent evolutionary research has found that regional branching and regional-related diversification is a very common form of incremental regional economic change. Regions diversify into related capabilities to allow for the partial reuse of regional resources. It is an efficient form of economic renewal.

Regional branching as a form of incremental regional change also provides one explanation as to why regional change is so often path dependent. We touched on path dependency in Chapter 2, where we established that it is one of the core concepts in evolutionary economic geography and has been studied in a great variety of ways. But we now know much more about resources and capabilities, and we can provide one more precise description of what path dependency actually is and why it seems to be so common.

The regional resources and how they are curated "suggest" a path of economic development that is very hard to diverge from, because branching processes into related activities is such an efficient form of change. Over time, regional economies incrementally branch out to develop related capabilities, as learning processes and curation alter the specificity of resources. This becomes a regional economic path. Consistent with the original path dependency idea, it is very difficult, if not impossible, to reverse this sequence of events and decisions. That is why it is path dependent: to diverge from the path of related change comes at a high cost for regions at best, and is impossible at worst.

Industrial change and structural change

It is empirically challenging to do research on all levels of our evolutionary perspective of regional economic production and how it changes across time in a region (resources–uses–capabilities). However, recent research has developed partial solutions to this challenge. The force of regional economic change is divided into radical and incremental. These concepts are very general, and from an evolutionary point of view they are unsatisfactory because they could refer to change at any of our levels.

The most common way of describing regional economic change, whether radical or incremental, is by tracking industrial change (Neffke *et al.* 2018). Industrial change describes how the uses of regional resources are distributed across output or use categories (industries or products) or which regional capabilities are achieved across time. Table 7.1 gives a typical picture of regional industrial change. It records the number of employees in different industries in the Gothenburg metropolitan region. The last column records the change between 2008 and 2018. For example, 1,115 fewer people were employed in manufacturing. Such numbers primarily record industrial change, because they measure, in a quite traditional way, how the regional labour resource is put to work at different times in specific industries.

Of course, one could imagine several other indicators of industrial change, for example the number of cars produced in Gothenburg today compared to historic volumes. Common to all of these indicators of industrial change is

Table 7.1 Regional industrial change: number of employees in the industries in Gothenburg and how it changed, 2008–18

Industry	**Employees 2018**	**Change 2008–18**
Agriculture, forestry and fishing	2,459	+732
Manufacturing; mining and quarrying	66,654	−1,115
Water supply, waste management, electricity supply	4,512	+444
Construction	36,462	+8,035
Wholesale and retail trade	68,248	+4,796
Transportation and storage	28,623	−94
Accommodation and food service activities	18,981	+4,357
Information and communication	26,721	+7,098
Financial and insurance activities	7,642	+384
Real estate activities	9,599	+2,338
Professional, scientific and technical activities, administrative and support services	81,365	+23,579
Public administration and defence	29,663	+7,930
Education	55,099	+11,265
Human health and social work activities	78,166	+11,177
Arts, entertainment and recreation, etc.	22,388	+3,419

Source: author's elaborations on data from Statistics Sweden.

that they record how different available regional resources are used at different points in time to achieve capabilities in a regional economy.

Indicators of industrial change deliver interesting information about regional economies and how they change. In Chapter 1, we described, using indicators about regional industrial change, how Gothenburg and Borås experienced a dramatic deindustrialization process, with the relative decline of manufacturing and growth of knowledge-intensive business services. This does not, of course, tell the whole story about the nature of economic change in Gothenburg and Borås in recent decades, but it certainly reflects the change that has taken place.

With the help of our evolutionary perspective, it is also easy to conclude that industrial change only focuses on economic change for a couple of levels, especially the capabilities and, to some extent, the derived resource uses. When capabilities and uses change, this is reflected in industrial change. However, industrial change has less to say about the real creation and curation of regional resources, and what alternative bundles could have been achieved by rebundling the derived regional uses. Industrial change tells a story about the achieved capabilities.

There are further problems that come with observing industrial regional change through an evolutionary lens. First, industrial change tends to exaggerate the foundations and speed of the economic change process itself (Neffke *et al.* 2018). Industrial change, such as a change in the production or the number of employees in an industry, can happen very quickly, even from one day to the next. If there were a sudden closure of an important regional firm, then there is rapid industrial change: production stops and people working in that industry in the region become unemployed. However, many of the regional resources that were utilized do not dissipate as quickly. They can still be used and recombined into new bundles. We already know that there is a limit to how long most resources can stay idle without deterioration, but for some time most of them are certainly candidates for other types of production.

There is also a statistical issue here. For many years, scholars have suspected that a substantial amount of the industrial change from manufacturing to services that economies in Europe and North America have experienced has to do with activities moving from one statistical code to another while using exactly the same regional resources. An example is the Swedish multinational telecom firm Ericsson, which was reclassified in 2017 from manufacturing to services by Swedish official statistics. Because Ericsson is such a big company, this has major implications for all kinds of data about the structure of the Swedish economy. The change reflects a real industrial change: Ericsson is far more focused on services now than it used to be, and probably uses different resources compared to 20 years ago. On the other hand, that process of change did not take place at some exact point in 2016–17. The speed of economic change is exaggerated if you look at industrial change only. There is no way that the regional resources that Ericsson employs could have changed that dramatically. In evolutionary economic terms, such a related industrial change is "shallow" because it has not meant a change in the regional resources themselves, and therefore little has altered in terms of the economic path that regions take, at least in the short run.

Second, to make matters even more complex, industrial change also sometimes underestimates the speed of change and how it alters the characteristics of regional capabilities already achieved. In 1960, Gothenburg produced cars and lots of employees worked in the car industry, which is still the case today. From that point of view, the car industry has not contributed that much to the immense industrial change process in the region. On the other hand, the content of this industry, in terms of the regional resources used and the uses derived from them, is totally different today. A car is a highly sophisticated technology, an infotainment machine, requiring advanced regional resources as well as the import of resource uses from other regions. There were many good things about cars in the 1960s, but they were not the technological wonders of today, and few of them were advanced entertainment machines. And as cars move into the electric paradigm, the content of the industry, as well as the industry itself, will change further. Little of this will be reflected in conventional indicators of industrial change.

Third, although industrial change shows fluctuations in regional resource use (for example labour), it does not tell us how regional resources themselves change and are curated over time. A regional productive capability can be temporarily maintained even if regional resources are not curated, but neglecting resource curation will compromise the future ability of the region to continue with certain productive bundles in the future. Regional complacency can of course be fatal: maybe not in the short run, but for the long-term regional ability to continue production.

Fourth, industrial change does not cover changes in regional capabilities that are not realized (what could be done but is not), nor changes in resources that are left unused or used in the wrong place. Tracking and realizing the potential for such change is a challenge, and it actually comes close to what Schumpeterian scholars expect entrepreneurs to do.

Overall, if industrial change, and how it relates to the evolutionary perspective of economic production, is examined in detail, it becomes obvious how partial an "industrial change" strategy is for describing regional economic change. It is convenient, but it is awkward to track regional economic change in this way, at least if it is the only strategy for analysing economic change.

Partly in response to these shortcomings, scholars have recently tried to take a closer and more systematic look at the extent to which industrial change really reflects changes in the regional resource repertoire, and how regional resources are used. Essentially, they try to answer the question of whether the observed industrial change in a region has also changed which resources are used and how they are used. If it has, then change is much more fundamental than a shift in or a rebundling of regional uses: it is change that also involves a change in the economic resources of regions, namely, regional structural change (Neffke *et al.* 2018).

Regional structural change describes the evolutionary fundamentals of economic change. Although industrial change can be quick, structural change normally takes much longer. As might be expected, regional structural change is closely linked to the way resource use and resource curation take place over time.

Gothenburg endured massive industrial change during the postwar era with the collapse of a globally successful shipbuilding industry, growing advanced truck and car industries and rapidly expanding business services, especially since 1990. There are good reasons to suspect that these changes also represent real structural change: a shift in the economy towards industries that, to a large extent, use a different set of regional resources. Deindustrialization (provided that term is accepted) and industrial change have put extreme demands on resource change.

Researching profound structural change is difficult (much more difficult than industrial change), and statistical systems are ill-equipped for it. Table 7.2 shows a partial element of this change: how Gothenburg's educational level has been pushed upwards over the years. This is a change in the regional skill resource. The table only covers a decade, but there is still a substantial increase in the number of people holding a tertiary (university) or doctoral degree. Thinking in this way, Table 7.1 represented industrial change but also obscured a lot of structural change. The growing industries in Gothenburg generally rely on a different set of human capital resources than the declining ones. In sum,

Table 7.2 Resource change: the highest educational levels of the population of Gothenburg and changes, 2008–18

Education	**Persons 2018**	**Change 2008–18**
Pre-secondary	115,011	−21,042
Secondary	287,427	+10,143
Tertiary	317,693	+81,152
Doctoral	12,083	+3,143

Source: author's elaborations on data from Statistics Sweden.

the transformation of the regional economy in Gothenburg over the last three decades spelled industrial change (changes in employment in different industries and in the products produced) but also, and maybe more importantly, structural change in the resource bases and the type of uses derived from them.

Relatedness and structural change

Measuring the degree of structural change taking place in regional economies – that is, to what extent new regional capabilities employ uses from a different set of regional resources than the old regional capabilities – is complicated. Regional economies include myriad changes in resources, uses and capabilities that take place all the time. How does one make sense of all that?

Over the last few years, researchers have tried to come up with new ways to achieve overall measures of regional structural change. Or rather, they have tried to figure out ways to measure change in the use of resources and whether new regional capabilities draw on uses of new and different regional resources, even though conventional ways of measuring economic change (industrial change) are not quite up to the challenge.

One workaround is to measure whether regional diversification takes place in existing related activities or if it takes place in activities that have very few links to previous capabilities. We have already defined "related economic activities" as those that are dependent on the uses of the same regional resources, or partially the same.

For example, among the most closely related activities to shipbuilding are (Eriksson, Henning & Otto 2016): manufacture of structural metal products; manufacture of other equipment related to mechanical engineering; shipping agents; and sea and coastal water transport. It makes intuitive sense that these are activities using many of the same resources as shipbuilding, although they do also draw on other resources. Some of the labour force in shipbuilding activities could deliver very productive uses to the "manufacture of other equipment related to mechanical engineering" or "shipping agent trade", for example. This makes the activities related: they depend on uses derived from the same resources.

The less a new regional capability is related to previous regional capabilities, by drawing on similar regional resources, the greater the degree of regional structural change taking place. The reason that this is true is that, by definition, a region needs to create new resources in order to accommodate a new, unrelated capability. This means that structural change reflects economic change in a region in a very profound way: from regional resources, via regionally derived uses, to the achieved regional capabilities. By contrast, unrelated regional change requires new regional resources to come in and do their job.

This way of looking at relatedness between activities has another consequence. If shared resource dependence is the crux of relatedness – and those capabilities that share use of resources are those that are more related – there must also be as many forms of relatedness as there are resources (Neffke & Henning 2013). So far, the consequences of relatedness for regional change have been explored from a couple of different angles, for example the skills of the labour force, scientific knowledge and production machinery and technology (Content & Frenken 2016). In contrast, we know little about how shared dependence on institutions affects regional diversification patterns today, but recent research is changing this (Trippl *et al.* 2020).

The consistent evidence from all this work is that regional economies frequently diversify into activities (capabilities) that are related to those that existed before. New work can incrementally branch out from the old, because it can draw uses from similar regional resources. Even in cases that require some resources to be created, related diversification is still an efficient way of diversifying an economy and creating novelty. Diversification into related activities limits the resource creation, discovery and curation processes that are necessary to achieve new regional capabilities. Related diversifications give regions a shortcut to achieving regional change.

Just about any economic history textbook will be well supplied with examples about (regional) branching into related activities. These examples range from the trivial to the surprising. At the trivial end of the spectrum, there are the incremental development efforts made by firms every day to tweak their products into new varieties and challenge the regional resources to deliver slightly different uses. On the incremental scale, if this results in a new regional capability being established, this is related regional diversification. This work is of course not trivial in itself, but it is theoretically trivial according to our evolutionary perspective. Firms do this all the time; it is their evolutionary raison d'être and part of their everyday business. So, when the rolling bearing manufacturer SKF develops a new variety of bearings for Volvo cars, it is most likely a sign of related diversification and incremental change at the micro scale. A new capability is established, but this partly uses the resources that SKF already have access to, delivering a capability that becomes an input that in turn delivers a use to another regional capability of Gothenburg, namely a fancy Volvo car.

There are more surprising examples of related diversification too. We have already reviewed one of these: the establishment of an Ericsson factory in the small textile town of Borås, close to Gothenburg. Although the access to experienced textile workers in Borås was certainly not the only reason why Ericsson was established there, it is an example of how regional resources (textile workers) can deliver uses to establish surprising new capabilities.

Most of this is also about scale. Whereas research has found that regions are much more likely to diversify into related activities, the degree of relatedness also matters. New activities have higher probabilities of entering if they have more related links to previous activities (Neffke, Henning & Boschma 2011). Relatedness is an important factor in explaining which types of capabilities regions are expected to diversify, but the degree of relatedness matters too.

In sum, related branching in regions is a perfect example of the general evolutionary axiom that "one thing leads to another", and therefore also of how path dependency occurs in regions. A series of related branching moves is a typical illustration of how regional path dependency works: because resources in certain fields are created, used and curated, and others not, this sets the conditions for the development of new regional capabilities.

Now, there is still a vital component missing in the story. Apart from the fact that resources may differ in their portability, so far the account has not been particularly geographical. Why is path dependency a regional phenomenon, and why does it seem to work differently in different regions?

Discussion points

1. Can there be incremental regional economic change without industrial change? Why/why not? Give a couple of examples.
2. When does the economic development of a region start? Give an example to illustrate your point.
3. What is a regional economic path?
4. Consider an example of related regional branching from your own region. How did that work?
5. When is radical regional economic change important? Under what circumstances can it be achieved?

8

Agglomerations

> If the perspective involves spatial concentration, however, examples of external economies of the technological kind become less elusive and are especially important with respect to learning and innovation over the long run.
>
> J. Parr, "Missing elements in the analysis of agglomeration economies", 162

What is happening within regions and agglomerations?

The first argument in Chapter 7 was that incremental change is common in regional economies. Such change varies in degree and can be studied on several different levels within regions: at the levels of resources, uses and capabilities. Second, incremental changes often take the shape of related regional diversification. In Jane Jacobs' words, new work develops from parent work in regions because of learning processes and what the old work "suggests" (Jacobs 1969). This is also one of the main reasons why so much regional development is path dependent. The regional resource repertoire and the specificity of regional resources condition the direction in which new work develops.

Resource building, diversification (i.e. the expansion of regional capabilities) and change are strong processes in the capitalist economy. Nevertheless, they seem to work in very different ways in different places, and regional economies look very different to one another. A key reason for this is that the regional resources themselves that are built, used and curated across time are very different from place to place. For example, informal institutions, such as the entrepreneurial spirit or cooperative norms, differ across different regions. This affects how and where resources can be combined into bundles and achieve capacities.

However, in order to understand why economic change looks so different in different regions, we need to explore another important geographical aspect that so far has been untouched. In this chapter, we investigate what happens in agglomerations, and how this effects how regional economic change happens. Later, the issue of what goes on between agglomerations, and how that affects regional change, is explored.

The main issue that we explore in this chapter is why regional change is essentially regional in nature. Certainly, regions have different resource repertoires, and some regional resources are not portable whereas others are, but is that all that differentiates regions that build resources and diversify more productively from those that do not? In this chapter, we explore ideas about what agglomerations of economic activities do to economic change and learn what research has to teach us in this regard.

Our evolutionary approach has been stylized so far, assuming that diversification processes take on the same forms in all regions, given their resource repertoires and the specificities of their main resources. Also, we have not considered whether resources are widely available in the region, or if they were appropriated by one or a just couple of firms. Regions are more than just places where regional resources are located and deliver uses that can be mechanically combined and recombined through organizational routines. They are also places where actors, entrepreneurs and firms discover paths to diversify, build resources to pursue those paths and do so in collaboration with other actors.

In a way, we touched upon this issue in Chapter 5, where we revisited the old argument from the management literature that putting resources to work also meant learning more about how resources could and should be used. Let us explore that argument a bit more closely from a regional point of view, by investigating how agglomerations and processes of regional learning-by-using are game changers when it comes to creating and curating regional economic resources.

In a language that economic geography (including evolutionary economic geography) shares with regional economics, a long line of research has investigated how agglomerations and regional economic structures – that is, the concentration of economic activities and the mix of firms that regional economies consist of – impact the cost structures, productivity and knowledge development of firms. In this book, we can only provide a glimpse into this debate and focus on the connections between agglomerations and our notion of industrial and structural change. Underpinning these admittedly partial arguments are the concepts, distinctions and theories put forward for example by:

- Marshall (1890), about the effects of specialized local economic environments;
- Jacobs (1969), about diversity in cities and diversification;

- Glaeser *et al.* (1992) and Ellison and Glaeser (1997), about different types of agglomeration effects and what characterize cities as economic environments;
- Krugman (1991), about increasing returns, agglomerations and the effects of regional integration;
- Porter (2000), about competitive advantage and regional clusters; and
- Frenken, Van Oort and Verburg (2007), about the effects of agglomerations of related firms (related variety).

Agglomeration advantages

The economic effects of co-location of firms can be divided into distinct classes that tell us something about the mechanisms by which the agglomeration advantages arise (Parr 2002). They are either advantages that arise from sources internal to the firm that are still constrained by space (economies of scale, scope and complexity), or are advantages that arise from sources external to the firm but internal to the region (localization economies, urbanization economies and activity-complex economies).

Theories in the Weberian tradition explained how geography and agglomeration affected firms' cost structures, for example, in terms of how regional market size contributes to achieving internal economies of scale. These are effects that are internal to the firm but constrained by space. Such effects and their sources are interesting and important, but here we are even more interested in the second category of benefits: those that are external to the firm but internal to the region.

(The theoretical connoisseur will note that much of the classical literature is not so precise when it comes to the distinction of sources of the agglomeration advantages: as something that arises from external economies or regional externalities. We can group these sources of agglomeration advantages together, because it does not affect our aim of looking at how the creation, use and curation of resources are facilitated in agglomerations, and how this links to regional change.)

BOX 8.1 CLUSTERS

Regional clusters are agglomerations of firms that are active in the same or similar industries. To what extent the firms need to be somehow connected in order to qualify as a regional cluster (something more than an agglomeration) is debated. In the original theory, a core feature of clusters was that the firms or industries were parts of the same value chain. The current literature is indecisive: often, links are assumed rather than observed. Yet, most scholars would agree that in order to qualify as a regional cluster there needs to be an agglomeration, and the firms need to share something or be linked. This sharing or linkage could be that the firms are parts of the same value chain, that they work with similar technologies or that they depend on the same regional institutions. Consequently, how clusters are defined is important. Different definitions also have very different theoretical and practical implications. See Delgado, Porter & Stern (2014).

Localization advantages capture benefits that accrue to firms within the same industry that co-locate. The most iconic distinction between the actual sources of these effects is derived from the works of Alfred Marshall (1890; also Parr 2002): formation of a pool of skilled labour (where a region becomes a "market for skill"); cooperation among firms in a value chain, knowledge spillovers and learning; and local growth of related services.

Urbanization advantages, or external economies of scope, are derived from the size effects that larger cities typically hold, such as a varied labour market, advanced knowledge infrastructure (e.g. universities and research institutes) and transportation possibilities with large cities acting as nodes in infrastructural networks (Neffke *et al.* 2011; Parr 2002).

Activity-complex advantages are not distinctly defined in the geographical literature but capture agglomeration effects from activities that are co-located and form parts of the same value chain (Parr 2002). To many geographers, such effects would be recognizable as components of regional clusters and are often tweaked into the category of localization advantages instead.

In recent decades, regional research has become more specific in terms of distinguishing between the agglomeration advantages that come with the size of regions, and those that have more to do with the virtues of regional economic variation (Glaeser *et al.* 1992). Jacobs' work on the economies of cities links two very important aspects: varied and innovative city environments and how existing work suggest new work.

Much of Jacobs' work dealt with cities and how, because of their richness in activities and ideas (economic variation), they are environments that foster innovation and branching into new activities. In the literature, the economic impacts of the economic variation of regions are therefore commonly known as Jacobs' advantages (or sometimes Jacobs' externalities) (Glaeser *et al.* 1992). Positive effects have been recorded for both productivity and firm survival (Neffke *et al.* 2011; Neffke, Henning & Boschma 2012).

In cities, many different activities of various types are compressed into relatively small spaces. The basic tenets of this class of agglomeration advantage is that diversified regions, often cities, provide plenty of regional inspiration to entrepreneurs and firms when they look for solutions to their particular problems. These can be compared to the localization benefits that deal with the effects of same-industry concentrations. In varied cities, however, knowledge diffusion is not characterized by the same-industry learning that Marshall talked about but rather by learning across traditional industry boundaries. This richness of information leads to particular types of learning and cross-industry combinations, where examples of problem solving from other contexts, such as in other industries, can be found in the regional vicinity.

Regions with a lot of economic variation often also have a hidden side, which allows for localization benefits to develop within varied bigger cities. Gothenburg, although certainly not one of the biggest cities in Europe, still offers some urbanization and Jacobs' advantages to its firms. Shared access to good infrastructure and, by Scandinavian standards, a varied labour market are two of them. On the other hand, it seems unreasonable to argue that these are the only regional effects. For the automotive industry, many of the important regional agglomeration benefits are surely those that come under the heading of localization advantages or benefits from regional specialization. Geely, the Chinese automaker and owner of Volvo Cars, has probably not invested in a huge vehicle technology research centre in Gothenburg because of the city's amazing economic variety, but because its specializations are in, or closely related to, the automotive industry.

This emphasizes an important point, which makes bigger cities difficult to compete with in terms of their evolutionary prospects: how can you compete with those regions that simultaneously generate localization, urbanization and Jacobs' advantages for their local firms?

Agglomerations and time: the dynamic movement

In fact, at times smaller and more coherent dedicated regional economies are more attractive to some firms and industries than large cities. Larger cities are more expensive on average and risk congestion effects. Large cities do contain more information about local resources that could be used to achieve new regional capabilities, but the information is also diffused across a wider range of regional actors. A large, diversified city will therefore be more difficult and costly to navigate than a smaller, coherent one. As a consequence, at stages of development or production when the advantages of bigger cities are not needed to achieve the desired capabilities, or when firms cannot identify relevant pieces of regional information fast enough, they do not need to locate to big cities (Neffke *et al.* 2011).

In other words, activities that find themselves in early life cycle stages (Chapter 2) appreciate the characteristics of varied regional economic environments more than activities in later and mature stages. Although more mature activities, for which technology has been standardized and price competition prevails, perform better in regions that provide them with localization economies (same-industry effects), younger and more innovation-intensive activities can make greater use of the ideas present in regions with higher industrial variation. They can also bear the financial burden of a high-cost environment better (Lundquist & Olander 1999; Duranton & Puga 2001; Neffke *et al.* 2011; Neffke, Henning & Boschma 2012).

This "dynamic" view of how different environments can be successful at different points in time and promote the growth of qualitatively different types of firms has been refined theoretically quite recently (Lundquist & Olander 1999; Duranton & Puga 2001). It is a major achievement, because in the evolutionary view the traditional treatment of agglomeration advantages was too static. It was concerned with how the properties of regional economies affect productivity at a specific point in time, rather than trying to integrate time and space to understand vacillations in regional successes. In essence, the traditional view of agglomeration benefits is good at explaining what the effects of the regional economic structure are on firms when agglomerations are already in place. This is of course important but not particularly evolutionary.

However, the divide between traditional views on agglomerations and more evolutionary approaches ought not to be exaggerated. An early clue to how the benefits of agglomeration could be made more dynamic originates in the conventional agglomeration literature itself, and in ideas about technological external economies (Parr 2002). These include spatial learning effects that have less to do with input costs than other forms of more traditional static agglomeration effects. And, as we have learned, some types of learning effects were part of Marshall's agglomeration frameworks. Knowledge spillovers were obvious and well-known features of the "Marshallian" same-industry agglomerations.

But again, recent advances in evolutionary research and related fields provide us with some helpful clues as to how to make the ideas of agglomeration advantages more dynamic and perhaps, ultimately, evolutionary.

The relatedness idea and regional economic coherence

To some, even these ideas about the qualities of agglomerations (same industry versus varied agglomerations) are not specific enough. For example, it seems strange to assume that diversity per se would be important for knowledge spillovers and innovation in regions. Surely, particular kinds of diversity in agglomerations must be especially important. After all, some activities are technologically closer to each other (Neffke, Henning & Boschma 2012). (Such arguments in evolutionary economic geography are inspired by the writings of Nooteboom 2000). And because economic actors do not conduct their search for inspiration and new solutions completely without prior expectations – that is, without an overall anticipation of where to find them – having related activities nearby may perhaps form a particularly important subcategory of regional variety effects (Boschma & Iammarino 2009).

This idea about the importance of regional-related variety has spurred a vibrant path of research over recent years. In essence, a growing literature argues that productive knowledge spillovers are more likely to take place between agglomerated, related activities in a region than between just any activities. Consequently, for economic outcomes, related variety (i.e. the regional variation in related activities) is important. So far, the evidence points to the presence of related variety being important for, for example, the survival of plants (Neffke, Henning & Boschma 2012), regional employment growth (Content & Frenken 2016) and innovation (Castaldi, Frenken & Los 2015).

Connoisseurs of agglomeration theories may find that this argument goes right to the heart of the classical variation argument; that variation in a regional economy is especially conducive to developing economies of scope. It follows that the chances of developing economies of scope must be far higher among activities that are related than among industries in general.

Now, these arguments stand and fall on a crucial issue: the definition of relatedness. Empirical research shows that depending on how related activities are defined, one risks ending up with very different results. In Chapter 7, it was shown that related activities are those that rely on using of the same, or partially shared, resources. The co-location of advanced manufacturing and knowledge-intensive producer services in Gothenburg is a typical regional agglomeration of related activities, which relies to a great extent on a shared labour resource in terms of technical and engineering skills.

Measuring relatedness empirically is not so straightforward. Early studies started to investigate relatedness as something that was captured through the traditional industry classification system (Frenken, Van Oort & Verburg 2007). Most countries in the world classify activities into industries according to a statistical nomenclature: for example, the NAICS (North American Industry Classification System) codes of North America or the NACE (Nomenclature statistique des activités économiques dans la Communauté européenne) codes of the EU (EU n.d.b). These classifications follow a tree-like structure, moving down from broad aggregates to ever finer categories of production, adding category digits to split up the aggregates and providing more detail. For example, at the most detailed level, the Swedish SNI (Standard för svensk näringsgrensindelning) industry classification system distinguishes between more than 800 different industries.

Figure 8.1 shows the Swedish classification system (which is based on the European NACE standard) in the case of textiles. The categories are divided into more detailed categories of trade. The point of defining related industries through this stepwise list is that industries under the same broad headings (e.g. "manufacture of textiles") are assumed to be related. The manufacture of carpets and rugs is assumed to be related to the manufacture of cordage, because they belong to the same "four-digit" level.

The classification of industrial activities is a convenient way of defining which activities and industries are (thought to be) related. It has also been shown that it makes empirical sense. However, it also comes with some weaknesses. For example, it is static: although it is incrementally revised at increasingly narrow time intervals, its fundamental structures – such as the basic distinction between manufacturing and services – were developed at the start of modern statistical systems during the second industrial revolution in the nineteenth century.

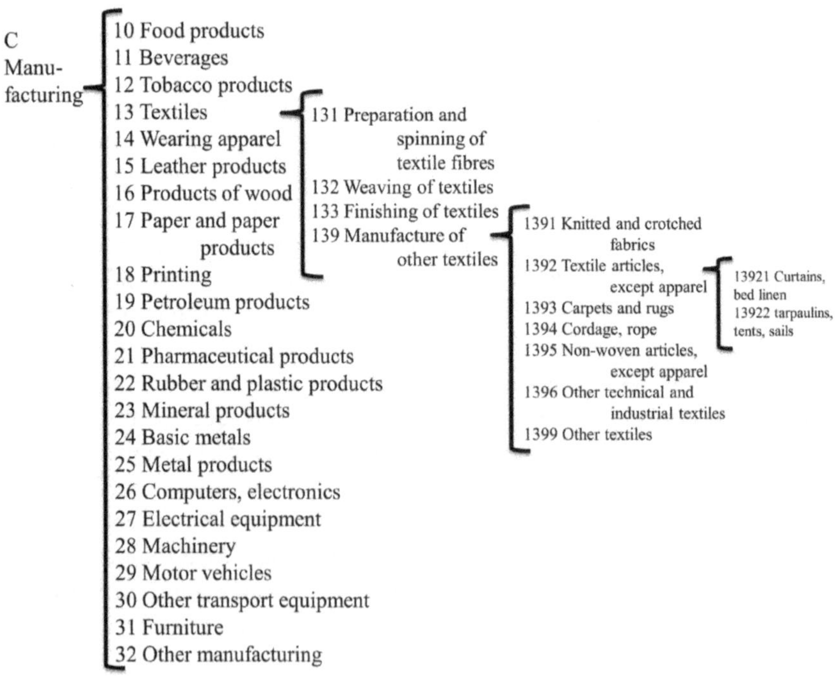

Figure 8.1 The hierarchical principle of industrial classification systems (Swedish example)
Source: Statistics Sweden, author's elaboration.

Hence, the distinction between manufacturing industries and services has proven difficult to overcome statistically, even if we know that these two parts of the economy are increasingly intertwined. One of the most emblematic manufacturing firms in Gothenburg, SKF, is a prime example of this. The firm has expanded its service repertoire, and although visitors to the firm's website can of course watch a picture of a modern factory producing rolling bearings, the page also has a tab for "services" as well as for "products".

As we noted in Chapter 7, our evolutionary perspective of production offers a better definition of related activities than the classification-based one. Related industries or activities are those that make use of (partially) the same regional resources.

Using this way of thinking and defining relatedness, the literature in economic geography has shown that regional production profiles – the productive capabilities that are achieved in regions – are on average coherent. This means that they consist of activities (industries) that draw, at least to some extent, on similar regional resources from which different uses are derived (Quatraro 2010; Kogler, Rigby & Tucker 2013; Neffke, Henning & Boschma 2011; Neffke *et al.* 2018). In short, related activities tend to agglomerate.

Again, the argument that regions are coherent in their capabilities' repertoire is not a new one in economic geography. However, the evolutionary framework offers a new way of measuring and explaining regional specialization patterns. This changes things, because it shows that regions not only specialize in separate industries or along value chains (Essletzbichler 2015) but also in activities that are related in terms of resources in ways that often transcend traditional industry classifications. The literature on the agglomeration of related activities has tried to measure, rather than assume, the links that tie firms in a region or a regional cluster more closely together.

In summary, it becomes important to note the conceptual distinction between the evolutionary use of:

- Relatedness: indicating if and how activities are dependent on the same, or partially the same, resources;
- Related variety: the extent to which the achieved capabilities of regions (what regions produce) are related; and
- Related branching: what happen when regional economies achieve new productive capabilities that depend on the uses of already established regional resources, that is, when new capabilities are related to the old ones.

In all, the comparatively static, traditional treatment of agglomeration advantages is of course useable and interesting, and investigating the empirical relevance of agglomeration advantages has a long history in geography research. But how do they translate into our evolutionary perspective? How do agglomeration advantages affect how resources are created and curated in regions? For the remainder of this chapter, we explore three evolutionary takes on agglomerations: (1) how agglomeration benefits affect regional change in terms of resource creation and curation; (2) how agglomeration benefits affect regional change in terms of establishing new bundles of uses and the establishment of new regional capabilities (industrial change); and (3) how agglomeration benefits affect regional change in terms of establishing new resources and the establishment of new regional capabilities (structural change).

Agglomerations, resource creation and resource curation

The conventional static accounts of how the properties of regional economies affect economic activities, for example in terms of productivity, do not entirely explain how economic change actually happens. However, this literature indicates that agglomeration advantages certainly have effects on regional resource creation and curation, and therefore on how regional economic change develops.

The first major insight arising from trying to merge the evolutionary perspective with arguments about the benefits of agglomeration comes when we realize that agglomeration benefits enable firms and other organizations to create and curate resources that could not be accomplished by one firm alone, or when firms are geographically isolated. This insight touches on the foundation of our evolutionary perspective and on some of the most fundamental aspects of economies, such as why there are regional labour markets that encompass people with specific skills that develop over time. Agglomeration effects matter not only to the performance of firms in terms of growth or labour productivity but also to which resources can be created and curated and how.

Localization benefits – those that stem from agglomerations of firms in the same industry – have already been explained as the effects sustained by a specialized regional environment. Such regional environments can benefit firms in terms of both creating and curating specialized resources for its core activity or industry. The specialization aspect is important. It means that the resources created by these agglomeration advantages come with higher degrees of specificity, and help to reinforce established paths but also renew and extend them by making it possible to establish recombinations with new and existing uses.

Table 8.1 notes some examples of how localization benefits affect both the creation of specialized resources and their curation. In terms of resource creation, a specialized regional setting should be increasingly attractive as a location alternative for a range of specialized resources. For example, Marshall highlighted that a specialized industrial district was attractive to workers in that industry, because "men seeking employment naturally go to places where there are many employers who need such skill as theirs and where therefore it is likely to find a good market" (Marshall 1890: IV.X.9). Specialized regions are also attractive to firms in that sector, because of the lower transportation and interaction costs with other firms in that sector or value chain.

The same is true for research organizations and other creators of specialized scientific knowledge. Co-location with firms that both rely on and co-develop knowledge lowers interaction costs and increases the opportunities for knowledge spillovers, but it also offers higher recruitment chances for skilled staff. It is common to find that specialized agglomerations of firms co-locate with tailor-made educational and research tracks in dedicated training and research facilities. In the old textile city of Borås, education in the field began in the 1860s and later developed into the Swedish School of Textiles, which today runs specialized educational programmes and undertakes advanced and specialized research. In Gothenburg, huge resources are invested into specialized R&D facilities in the next-generation automotive sector. Such investments are not cheap. A well-established and coherent regional production profile, however, may make it easier to attract capital to the region.

It is harder to explain how regional institutions that help to drive regional businesses forward are established, other than that they tend to grow out of a long historical development. Theories highlight the presence of trust between regional actors as a transaction cost-reducing mechanism in (specialized) industrial districts (Amin 2003). However, dedicated and specialized institutions, such as norms and habits in specific industries and regions, can also be problematic, stall change and diversification and reinforce regional lock-in (Grabher 1993). Conservative attitudes and complacency, which puts too much trust in the future competitiveness of a strong regional specialization, will at best postpone change and at worst destroy the chance to redirect the uses derived from regional resources to new applications.

It is easier to see how specialized regional policies are established. Promoting regional specialization and deepening successful specialization has been on the agenda of many regional development agencies during recent years. At the beginning of the 2010s, the Västra Götaland regional government (of which Gothenburg is a part) made its regional priorities clear by highlighting "urban future", "the marine environment and the maritime sector", "transport solutions", "green chemistry and bio-based products" and "life science" as the region's five clusters. Even if a certain amount of regional marketing and political ambition are often present in defining regional specializations for strategic economic development, they also suggest areas of priority to the region's policy-makers. We return to this discussion in Chapter 11, where we talk more about the connections between evolutionary economic geography and policy initiatives based on the EU's smart specialization framework.

Localization advantages can also be offered in more direct pecuniary ways, for example by sharing costs for the purchase of specialized fixed capital and creating specialized infrastructure. A classic argument in the agglomeration literature is that firms in regions that develop localization advantages are given the chance to create external economies of scale that cut their production costs (Asheim 2000). This is of course theoretically true, but maybe more important from an evolutionary point of view is the fact that it also allows firms to share costs that enable them to develop economies of scope. This creates opportunities to achieve new regional capabilities.

Regional resources also need to be curated to stay viable for future use in productive bundles and to remain attractive candidates for new bundles of resource uses in order to achieve new regional capabilities. In such a context, the localization advantages created include sharing costs for fixed capital and infrastructure maintenance, as well as lowering transaction costs for collaboration between individuals, firms and research institutes in the region.

It is not difficult to understand why localization benefits help regions to establish additional specialized resources in regions and to facilitate the curation of specialized resources that are already in place. We can reason analogously when it comes to urbanization and Jacobs' benefits to agglomeration – benefits to firms arising from the variation of technologies and types of capabilities in regional economies – and the size of the economies (Table 8.2). The evolutionary strength of regions characterized by urbanization/Jacobs' benefits

Table 8.1 Localization advantages, regional resource creation and regional resource curation

Resource	Creation	Curation
Specialized fixed capital	Procurement (shared costs)	Maintenance (shared costs)
Specialized labour force	Attraction	Competence development (shared costs, labour mobility)
Specialized infrastructure	Building (shared costs)	Maintenance (shared costs)
Financial capital	Attracting financial and venture capital	
Firm agglomeration	Attraction (lower interaction costs)	Collaboration (lower costs)
Research organizations and other creators of specialized scientific knowledge	Attraction (lower interaction costs)	Collaboration (lower costs)
Institutions	Specialized regional institutional building	Collaboration (lower costs)
Policy	Specialized regional institutions	Collaboration (lower costs)

Table 8.2 Urbanization/Jacobs' advantages on regional resource creation and curation

Resource	Creation	Curation
A varied labour force	Attraction	Competence development (shared costs, labour mobility)
Infrastructure	Building (shared costs)	Maintenance (shared costs)
Financial capital	Attracting financial and venture capital	
Firm agglomeration	Attraction	
Research organizations and other creators of scientific knowledge	Attraction (lower interaction costs)	Collaboration (lower costs)

comes with the vast resource repertoire that such regions are able to create and curate. Because of their size, such regional economies will be attractive to many firms because of their large regional markets, supporting a varied regional economy and a varied and high-skilled regional labour market. The same goes for research organizations and other creators of scientific knowledge that are often (but not always) located in bigger cities. Bigger regions also enjoy better regional infrastructure, such as highways, airports, ports and railways.

One could argue that specialized regions develop agglomeration benefits that also allow for the establishment of low-specificity resources. A textile city may provide enough demand for the construction of an airport or internet infrastructure that would benefit all kinds of trades. This is true for some types of general infrastructure, whereas pure regional agglomeration, of any economic kind, will generate benefits for its establishment. However, this type of effect would fall into the urbanization category. The airport is built because of the size of the textile city rather than because of its specialization. Again, bigger cities seem attractive, as they are the ones that are able to create and curate both a range of specific and general resources in the same region.

We have treated agglomeration advantages, whether small or sizeable, all under one umbrella because the logics behind enormous and moderate agglomeration benefits are basically the same. But there are of course considerable degrees in scale. Curating the regional resource of an international airport requires sharing costs on a huge scale, and curating a varied labour market requires the co-location of potentially thousands of firms. On the other hand, it might be sufficient with the co-location of three firms to sustain a local specialized labour market on a modest scale. The co-location of a couple of firms is an indicator that there are some kind of agglomeration benefits. Gothenburg exemplifies, in theoretical terms, agglomeration benefits by the same logic as New York or Beijing, but on a much-reduced scale.

Localization advantages, related activities and incremental industrial change

Traditional opinions on agglomeration benefits have focused on how the properties of locations affect firm performance. We have already interpreted these accounts according to our evolutionary perspective by discussing how agglomeration advantages affect the creation and curation of different types of regional resources. Classification of the different types of agglomeration advantage, and understanding what they do in terms of resource creation and curation, is important. Even more importantly, and definitively more interesting to us, is what this actually means in terms of economic change.

In other words: what kinds of regional economic change do the different agglomeration advantages prepare for? How do different kinds of regional economic environments offer suggestions for future work and enable their realization from the regional resources that have been established?

Sometimes, comparatively specialized regional environments, such as Borås or even parts of the economy in Gothenburg, seem to be static. This is not necessarily true because they certainly change within their specializations. Overall, the literature teaches us that the localization benefits generated in specialized regional environments are particularly good at creating and curating resources that are in line with the general specialization of the region. This is because these types of agglomeration benefits create and curate resources that come with a relatively high degree of specificity. That is, regions that are not big cities and are somewhat specialized experience economic change, but the direction of change for them is more limited than for the bigger cities and is path dependent.

Consider the Swedish School of Textiles in Borås, or the new research centre of automaker Geely in Gothenburg. These facilities will undoubtedly reinvigorate the local industry specialization and launch new, related, innovative products or processes. From our evolutionary point of view, regional actors will discover new uses to establish new bundles, including those already drawn from existing regional resources. There will be change and growth, but it will probably exemplify regional path dependency.

There is a chance, of course, that resources promoted by localization advantages will precipitate radical innovations that break new paths and are game changers in all respects. This can happen. But it is unlikely, and it is probably not why these resources were created in the first place. It is more likely that they will come up with great innovations and suggest recombinations of resource uses within reasonable limits of the specialization of the region.

The blessings of regional localization advantages and prospects for path-dependent change also come with a potential curse. If the specialized recombinations at some point become economically unviable, or if they run out of technological steam, there are few low-friction areas to turn to in the regional economy. If the resources gradually become increasingly specific, the risk is that the development paths of specialized regions will reach an eventual end point. This results in a lock-in of the regional economy, and radical economic change is required. This could either be the economic end (for that region) or serve as an impetus for an economic revolution.

Lock-in is a situation in which reasonably related diversification paths simply come to an end, either because the regional resources are too specific or because the diversification alternatives are not economically viable. The reasons why some regions end up in these situations could also be sociological and institutional, such that the regional actors discovered too late that they were heading for the "end of the line" (Grabher 1993). Such end points represent some of the most challenging situations for coherent regional economies and put enormous pressures on the need to achieve radical change through resource creation.

Gothenburg was on the brink of a disastrous lock-in during the 1970s and early 1980s. Its shipbuilding specialization had reached its end point, and with increasing deindustrialization things were not particularly promising for other types of manufacturing either. However, radical change later provided new opportunities, as the technology shift led to the computerized industrial revolution that instigated new opportunities for emerging regional resources in the city. Other traditional manufacturing towns across Europe and the USA were not given similar opportunities to create attractive regional resources and reorient towards growing industries and applications. Instead, lock-in forced radical change for the worse.

In trying to avoid lock-in by becoming entrenched in capabilities based on high-specificity resources, diversification into related activities has proven an especially important route for regional change for coherent economies. Many studies have shown that activities that are more related to the industries already present in a region also have a higher chance of future entry (Neffke, Henning & Boschma 2011; Content & Frenken 2016). Instead of deepening a regional specialization through localization advantages, this is again an argument about incremental diversification and the rebundling of resource uses into new, related combinations. And the more related activities present, the higher the chance of forming new productive bundles that achieve new regional capabilities. In coherent but not completely specialized environments, the chance of developing relevant combinations from existing regional resources are simply higher.

So what does evolutionary research teach us about the type of evolutionary change that the different kinds of agglomeration advantages on average prepare for? (See Figure 8.1 for a summary.)

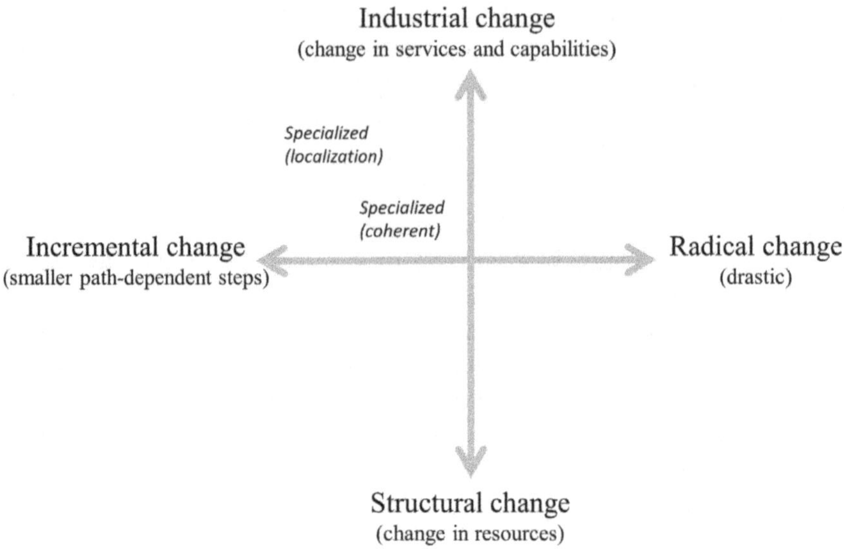

Figure 8.2 Agglomeration advantages and dominating types of change (1)

Agglomeration advantages in specialized regions mainly prepare for regional incremental industrial change. In such regions, actors learn about related alternatives for the combination and recombination of resource uses in their vicinity and from actors in the same industry. Specific resources are established and curated. The specialized resources and the dedicated business climate of some regions affects the potential for future combinations of regional resource uses too: many specialized regions carry huge potential for developing new combinations of regional resource uses in the future.

The agglomeration advantages of coherent regional economies also prepare for regional incremental industrial change, but with a greater scope for change. In such regions, actors learn about related alternatives for combination and recombination of resource uses from actors in related activities in their vicinity. It is probable that highly specific resources are established and curated, but research is not yet precise enough on this point. However, we do know that this type of regional change constitute empirically important processes of regional diversification into related capabilities.

Variation advantages, incremental and structural change

One of the key arguments concerning varied regional environments is that they offer regional alternatives for the recombination of resource uses that are available in the region. This speaks to the virtue of cities as places where many different uses and capabilities are confined to a tight space, allowing economic actors to monitor all kinds of solutions that others develop.

Urbanization and Jacobs' advantages also enable regions to sustain a wide repertoire of lower-specificity resources. In that sense, they are richer resource environments in which learning can take place, and from where new regional capabilities can branch out from general, as well as highly specific, regional resources.

Here too, we can formulate a proposition about how agglomeration advantages affect the characteristics of regional change (Figure 8.2):

- Populous regions have a greater capacity to create and curate non-specific resources that provide opportunities to derive uses for many different activities and create new ones that can shift the economic development path in new and unexpected ways.
- In varied (diverse) regions, the presence of uses derived from regional resources provides a greater regional repertoire that allows for recombinations because actors are more likely to learn about them, observe them in their vicinity and monitor their development. These are examples of how Jacobs' agglomeration effects, based on presence of variety, affect the potential for incremental change and a multitude of recombining and branching experiments in high-variety regional economies.

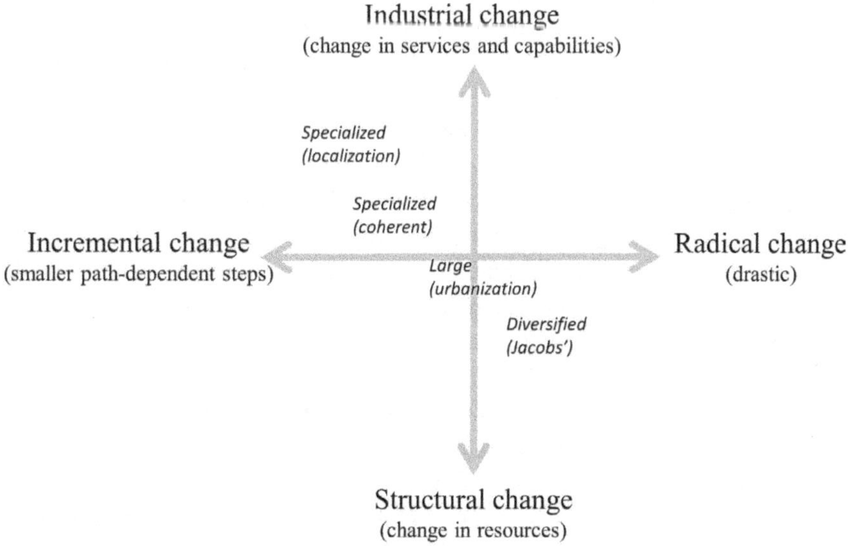

Figure 8.3 Agglomeration advantages and types of change (2)

It is important to remember that the changes the different agglomeration advantages prepare for are more about types of change than about types of regions. As discussed above, path-dependent change can occur within populous cities, as it has done in Gothenburg. However, big regions tend to contain more paths, and most regions do not consist of only one type of change. Change occurs all the time in regions and takes different forms. However, it is unlikely that small and specialized regions experience radical change as a result of agglomeration advantages; change has to be created by other means.

How regional economic change sometimes works: radical change where agglomerations have little impact

So far, we have assumed that agglomerations – the co-location of activities – are already in place to generate different kinds of benefits that in turn help regions to create and curate their resources. Because of its empirical importance, evolutionary economic geography has traditionally been mostly concerned with incremental change and related branching, based on existing regional resources and their uses. Related diversification is a strong force of regional incremental change and complements the idea of how evolution is normally thought of: as a stepwise process of novelty introduction and selection, where retention (the paths) puts limits both on the speed of change and its direction.

However, there are other forms of economic change (see Chapter 2). We have already mentioned radical and structural change. If these coincide, it leads to great shifts in regional economies. This is not common, but it does happen. When it does, it is all the more significant (Enflo & Henning 2016).

There are cases in which agglomeration advantages promote these radical shifts, for example when drastic recombinations instigated by Jacobs' benefits give rise to new industries in unexpected ways. However, epic radical moments and processes of change have less to do with agglomerations or even with predefined spatial structures at all. Radical change that coincides with dramatic structural change generates completely new regional resources, new regional resource uses and the achievement of new regional capabilities, which are changes at all levels of the evolutionary perspective (see Figure 8.2).

Can we predict where such radical changes are more likely to take place? Or are they the result of chance? From a social science point of view, chance is not a particularly convincing explanation, because change in societies is not stochastic. In many cases, "chance" is a metaphor for our lack of knowledge.

Three examples from the economic history and economic geography literature can offer some illumination:

- Technological change and radical innovation create a shift in which regional resources can be seen as productive, important and forming the base for new regional capabilities;
- Technological change and radical innovation create a shift in which new types of production (industries) arise for which there exist no specific resources, but these have to be created; and
- New resources are created in regions, from which new uses can be derived and new regional capabilities achieved in activities (industries) that exist outside the region but have no related friends in the region.

A prime source of radical change is massive technological development. During the industrial revolution, new technologies were developed that partly changed the dependency between firms and the resources in their locations. For example, with the diffusion of steam power, production became less dependent on direct access to water power (Berger, Enflo & Henning 2012; Enflo & Henning 2016). But new resources (fixed capital) needed to be created to take advantage of this way of producing power. By creating those, new uses could reach new regions. This process served to diffuse manufacturing in Sweden. A contemporary example is how the IT server halls of tech giants, which require constant cooling, are located in peripheral regions in the north of Sweden. Suddenly the cold climate, which has not been a productive regional resource for hundreds of years, becomes useful. This is not the only regional resource needed to open up the server halls, but it is a necessary one.

BOX 8.2 THE INDUSTRIAL REVOLUTIONS

The industrial revolutions are (extended) periods of great technological, institutional and social change. The second industrial revolution took place in the second half of the nineteenth century. Many scholars argue that computers are at the core of a new industrial revolution. However, the timing and force of a third (or fourth) industrial revolution is debated. See Schön (2010) and Freeman & Louça (2001).

With technological revolutions, new, innovative products are also introduced, some of them requiring access to completely new regional resources. Today, technological sophistication in knowledge-intensive services has created a dependence on new types of skills. In general, throughout history and at particular times, technological discontinuities have created a new playing field for regions, industries and firms, as new regional resources and uses become important to the achievement of new and innovative regional capabilities. In sum, industrial revolutions affect radical regional change (but not that often) (Schön 2010).

To further understand the locational consequences of the industrial revolutions, we can turn to a classic idea in economic geography: windows of locational opportunity (Storper & Walker 1989; Boschma 1997). This idea links to concepts such as technology shifts and industrial revolutions and to the argument that there are times when achieving new capabilities in regions is not linked to the previous resource repertoire, because the new capability requires new resources to be created. In such phases of economic development, which are rare but important, many locational choices are possible for a new activity, and the choice is not conditioned by previous activities. The windows of locational opportunity are open. In such contexts, firms are not mere takers of regional resources, they are also instrumental in establishing them. Firms can at times build new resources in regions, derive new uses and achieve new capabilities.

Essentially, this is a question of establishing new regional economic paths and of completely escaping path dependency. The literature on new path development is young but growing, and it discusses how regional resources can be built as well as the role of agents in establishing such new paths (Isaksen & Trippl 2017). The establishment of new paths in regions – understood as establishing capabilities based on resources and uses that are completely new to the region – requires two things from our evolutionary point of view: (1) resource creation, and (2) early learning-by-using of the resources.

That is, given that enough investments are made, completely new but specific regional resources can be created. However, some of the most important resources in economies are more difficult and expensive than others to create, for example productive institutions and specific and experience-based human capital. In Porter's (1990) terms, these resources are hard to imitate and therefore provide the basis for long-term competitive advantage. Infrastructure, less specific human capital and fixed capital are categories that are easier to create, as long as the investment can be made.

Recent examples of processes where regions and countries completely shifted their economic development paths using these strategies are the current rise of some Asian regions to assume top economic positions, achieving regional capabilities that until recently were reserved for the "industrialized" Western economies. One especially interesting story is the one of the main competitors to Gothenburg's once proud shipbuilding industry: the South Korean shipyards. From humble beginnings in the 1970s and without the presence of any of the high-specificity resources actually needed to build modern state-of-the-art ships, South Korean shipyards have developed into some of the most important players on the world market. Through targeted investments by government, learning and resource importation, South Korean regions were able to achieve completely new capabilities, derive productive uses and experience thoroughly radical structural change (Hassink & Shin 2005).

Regions can, therefore, escape their economic past and break new paths. However, the odds are against them. Although radical and structural change can be achieved, decades of research in economic geography has shown how powerful regional resources are. They cannot be created easily nor be imitated, and they are expensive to create and curate.

Agency

Finally, who has the power to introduce change in a region? Who has the agency to make change happen? Recent evolutionary research shows that relatively greater incremental pushes in terms of structural change are achieved primarily by entrepreneurs and firms that come from outside the region. It seems harder to accomplish structural change from within and with firms that are already settled and embedded in the existing regional specializations. These findings complement our previous arguments about the different kinds of change that agglomeration benefits prepare regions for (Neffke *et al.* 2018).

In fact, research shows that firms that enter new regions and instigate structural change are on average better embedded in their home regions with a better network than in the regions they enter. This has to be a sign of the diffusion of routines, knowledge and/or financial capital that enable new entrants to build new resources in the regions that they enter into, or the import of resources from other regions.

Although recent evolutionary research has focused on firms and entrepreneurs as "agents of change", it is important not to dismiss or forget the role that government plays in promoting regional change. This role is stressed by institutional economic geography when it comes to creating innovation and establishing new technology paths in regions. It is difficult to give an overall account of the importance of governments and policy for regional change. Governments and policies are diverse and do very different things in different regions.

Yet, we have already noted how important the public sector is when it comes to creating and curating regional resources (Chapter 6). Education of the labour force is one example: there are few economies where this is left entirely to the market.

When it comes to instigating radical shifts, aspects of agency are even more complex. However, research tends to show that governments are often involved in these shifts and in building the new resources needed to make them happen in many, if not most, cases. This is true for South Korea, Sweden, China and the USA. This does not mean that governments can achieve economic shifts on their own. Although they have important roles to play in creating and curating regional resources, they notoriously fail when it comes to deriving the right uses from them and in achieving the right capabilities. Therefore, this is often, in one form or another, left to entrepreneurs and firms.

To break the bonds of regional path dependency, connections to the "outside" seem to be critically important for radical regional change (Isaksen 2014). In Chapter 9, we therefore continue to open up the evolutionary processes in regions to influences from outside.

Discussion points

1. Are there differences between agglomeration benefits that have to do with costs versus those that have to do with knowledge? Give examples of both.
2. Have cities always been attractive places for economic activities?
3. How did the importance of agglomerations change with digital technologies?
4. What is the future of small regions? Will they be able to compete with big regions that offer both advantages of size and pockets of specialization?

9

Evolutionary economic geography and time geography

> In the factory, men, machines, and materials form bundles by which components are connected and disconnected. In the office, similar bundles connect and disconnect information and channel messages.
>
> T. Hägerstrand, "What about people in regional science?", 149

Globalization, regional resource uses and time geography

So far, the evolutionary perspective has acquainted us with a rather peculiar version of the world and of economic production, where the most important resources are linked to space (they are localized), and where all uses are derived from resources located in the same region. In theoretical terms, we have created a regionally endogenous model, and one that is actually not too far from the evolutionary "self-reliant" or territorially isolationist models of growth that have been influential in geography and innovation studies over the last 20 years.

For example, we have taken for granted that the car producer in Gothenburg only made use of resources in the region and their regionally derived uses in order to achieve the regional capability of car production. Links to other regions were not needed, neither in production nor in product or process development. So, if our first simplification of how production happens within the car industry was not already a stretch, the assumption that regions are "self-sufficient" in terms of resources and uses to achieve their capabilities is maybe even more so. In fact, we have already concluded that some of the most important forces for economic change in regions originate from outside the region itself. Additionally, there is globalization.

Regional economies are today part of global chains of production and are not isolated production islands (Coe *et al.* 2004). Intuitively we know this: the transportation of goods, people and information have become faster, cheaper and safer since the second industrial revolution. The telephone and the internet have dramatically changed the way we interact across space. Very few economic activities, from the local garage to transnational corporations, from the local supermarket to the global suppliers of knowledge-intensive services, are left untouched by the global forces of change influencing where economic activities can be located and how firms go about their business.

There are at least two implications of this development for evolutionary economic geography that are far less intuitive. The first is a "regional paradox of globalization". The more linked regions become through globalization, the more economic activities have concentrated regionally within the countries that participate in globalization (Rosés & Wolf 2018). As we found in Chapter 1, distance matters less, but places matter more. Essentially, the paradox could be resolved by looking at the impact of agglomeration advantages (Krugman 1991; Rosés & Wolf 2018). If transport costs are no longer a dominating issue, and firms and people are given the choice to locate in dense regions and enjoy all the advantages of agglomerations, or alternatively to locate to sparse and peripheral regions, why on earth would they prefer the sparse and peripheral alternative? (Provided that the agglomerations do not come with completely devastating costs, which some of them actually do.)

Second, the fact that globalization comes with a new division of labour and new patterns of regional specialization is without question and is a well-established fact in the international trade and international business literatures.

Yet, the issue of how exactly globalization links to evolutionary processes of (regional) economic change has been left largely unexplored by evolutionary scholars. This could be because scholars have already been occupied with working out the regional fundamentals of the approach without taking the complexity of globalization into account (Chapter 2). There has also been an absence of a good micro-oriented conceptual framework to handle the changing relationships between distance versus place that come with globalization. In sum, it has been very difficult to get a systematic grip on how better and cheaper communications have affected resource building, use and curation in regions. The result is that there has been no real link between the region-centred approaches and global approaches in economic geography.

A fundamental question is: how has economic globalization changed the introduction of novelty, retention and selection in regional economies? To explore answers to this question, we need to merge evolutionary economic geography with time geography. We have already (in Chapter 3) explored what time geography is and what it can contribute. The rest of the book explores how we can complement the "original" evolutionary perspective with time geography to explain better how flows of input goods, flows of services and knowledge flows between regions matter to how and when regions are able to achieve new capabilities.

By integrating evolutionary economic geography with time geography, we find that globalization changed the evolutionary economic development of regions because it revolutionized the way that the use of resources can be traded and then come to be included in productive bundles to achieve productive capabilities in other regions. This is how globalization changed the regional evolutionary economic world.

Generalizing "individuals" to "resources" in time-space

Although the early accounts of time geography talked about "things" and individuals, the time geography approach became almost exclusively individual-centred. Hägerstrand himself mostly used individuals' coordination in time-space as examples of how time geography could be applied, although he envisioned a broader socio-economic web model than one that is only concerned with individuals. In order for it to become an approach that furthers the understanding of economic evolution, more "things" and "resources" need to be added to the time geography picture.

If we were to take a more general stance and require resources to be coordinated in time-space to achieve capabilities (projects), the time geography language becomes compatible with the ideas of evolutionary economic geography. Further, it provides a component missing in evolutionary economic geography, namely a language to assess how globalization has affected how resources are created, used and curated in regions, and how uses derived from localized regional resources are increasingly traded.

In fact, we snuck in some of the time geography language into the evolutionary ideas of production when we assumed that one of the most important roles of firms in the economy is that they organize bundles of uses derived from regional resources to achieve a regional capability. Let us start by having a look at the simplest bundle situation, which we already know partially from Chapter 3.

How time geography constraints affect the creation, use and curation of regional resources

Time geography sets out three different categories of restrictions that limit how the bundles can be composed in time-space. How this affects the evolutionary change of regional economies starts with the definition of the "region" itself. In a functional definition of the region (Chapter 1), or in our case more precisely the labour market region, the region is in fact often thought of as the average worker's daily prism. The functional region consists of the potential production sites (factories and offices) that can be accessed by the average individual, with the individual still getting home at a reasonable time in the evening. In that sense, the "regional" development discussion rests on assumptions that can be easily connected to how capability restrictions limit the daily prism of the workforce. This can be seen in any city of size. In Gothenburg, the entire commuter system is built around the logic of expanding the prisms of the working population, so that they can commute between the city centre or the major industrial facilities from the suburban residential areas.

The reason for merging evolutionary economic geography with time geography is that this argument can be generalized and is relevant to more classes of resources than just labour. It is in fact relevant to all classes of portable resources. All resources and derived uses do not need to be back at their original sites in the evening, but they still have limits to how they can be transported and coordinated in time-space, and where and when they can participate in bundles to achieve a capability. Achieving a particular economic capability is a geographical process because time-space restrictions (capability, coupling, authority) affect where resources can be used and the uses that can be derived from resources.

Let us first examine more precisely what the time geography constraints do to the creation, use and curation of regional resources, and thus make the conditions for bundling processes very different in different places (Table 9.1).

Capability constraints impose portability limits on resource creation, use and curation. Some regional resources are more affected than others by the capability constraints. All resources that have a basic degree of portability (Chapter 3) are affected by costs, access and quality of transportation alternatives, or in Hägerstrand's terms, the properties of the tools available for them to overcome distance and at what speed.

Fixed capital, financial capital and individuals are all resources where capability constraints limit the creation and use of a regional resource, and limit how and where they can participate in productive bundles and for how long. Resources that are associated with people (such as skills) mark a category of

Table 9.1 Some examples of what time geography constraints do to regional resources

	Resource creation	**Resource use**	**Resource curation**
Capability constraints	Portability	Portability	
Coupling constraints		Specificity, portability	Portability
Authority constraints	Appropriability	Appropriability	Appropriability

resources that are particularly vulnerable to limits in portability set by the capability constraints. In normal cases, as the initial contributions on time geography made clear, people are tied to starting in a particular place in the morning and returning back to it in the evening.

Creating a regional labour resource means that a host of time-space constraints have to be overcome, or at least decreased, and this can be achieved in two main ways: by creating a regional resource of labour by the "import" of individuals through migration (Chapter 6); and by creating a regional resource of labour by enlargement of the daily prisms of individuals, for example through easier commuting.

Today, all over the world, governments spend huge sums investing in regional infrastructure to "enlarge" their labour market regions. The preferred strategy is not to build motorways but railroads. Gothenburg recently embarked on a huge railway infrastructure project: a railway tunnel below the city encompassing three new commuter stations estimated to cost €2 billion. In practice, such projects reduce capacity restrictions and enlarge daily prisms to create a larger regional labour market (size) but also to facilitate for the building of new, niche labour specialties with a high degree of specificity.

Coupling constraints are requirements on the bundle duration in order to achieve a capability. In some industries and for some regional resources, the daily presence between specific hours at a factory (resource physical co presence time and space) is crucial in order to accomplish a capability. For example, truck manufacturing in Gothenburg comes with relatively high coupling constraints. Resources need to be physically present at very specific points in time and for relatively extensive durations in order to achieve the regional capacity to build the truck. This creates extreme demands on the organizational routines: work sequences have to be planned in detail to make the time-space coordination possible. In other industries, the coupling constraints on resources are lower. Parts of the advanced service industries require very little co-presence and coordination of resources in time and space. At specific points during the development of a software package, for example, a project has of course to be coordinated in time-space. Between those points, however, achieving the capacity to develop the software is met with low coupling constraints.

This suggests a couple of theoretical points. When achieving a regional capability puts requirements on a long bundle duration (high coupling constraints), the resource will be locked to this use and cannot take part in alternative uses. In practice, this impacts the specificity of a resource: it cannot be used to develop economies of scale and scope in other settings. Coupling constraints also impact the portability of resources and their potential prisms. If a resource, such as an individual, is locked into a bundle to achieve a specific capability for a certain time, this will limit her prism for the rest of the period and limit the chance that she will be able to participate in other bundles in other places. This is not that surprising, but the main lesson is what happens when coupling restrictions change. We come back to this in Chapter 10.

Authority constraints in time-space are maybe not the first thing that come to mind when discussing regional economic resources, but they constrain the creation, use and curation of the regional labour force in important ways. First, authority constraints are tightly linked to resource appropriability. The power over domains influences how resources are created, used and curated in real terms. Governments may block individuals, or other resources, from entering their domains, thereby affecting how regional resources are created and used. In real life, authority constraints affect whether resources can be appropriated at all by regional actors.

The easiest example is the way in which migration laws and regulations create authority constraints that affect both the creation and use of the regional labour force. In fact, creating a regional labour force (or at least parts of it) through migration is increasingly constrained by myriad authority constraints. This is certainly true between countries and especially between continents. Also, historically, low authority constraints to migration within countries could not even be taken for granted. In Sweden, free domestic travel was only introduced with the second industrial revolution in the second half of the nineteenth century.

The same goes for resource use: governments, firms and institutions restrict a resource's movements in time-space, and thereby in practice condition whether, for example, a resource really becomes a regional resource in its use or whether it should be seen as an organizational resource. Infrastructure might seem a very general resource, but if domains limit access to it, it becomes less so. Safety concerns, for example, limit the accessibility of resources to domains. In 2019–20, many Western countries raised concerns about the conditions of use among the huge Chinese telecom manufacturer Huawei's products, with some countries banning their use in infrastructure construction. Whether they are legitimate concerns or illegitimate barriers to trade, these restrictions serve as perfect examples where the creation of regional infrastructural resources (from a specific manufacturer) is made more difficult, more expensive or delayed in time by authority constraints.

Cars again

As a final step in exploring how time-space constraints condition when and where productive bundles of resource use can be formed to achieve a regional capability, let us merge the evolutionary perspective into the graphical representations of time geography.

In Chapter 3, we settled for a simplified version of car making based on five regional resources: specialized labour, machines, infrastructure, research and materials. Figure 9.1 resembles the spirit of the time geography figures that Hägerstrand drew in the 1970s (see Figure 3.6 in Chapter 3). In Figure 9.1, a restricted list of essential resources for car production are listed in the Gothenburg region. These resources are used as long as production continues (the bundle). Now we apply the insights from previous chapters in the following way:

- The project – to achieve a regional capacity (making a car) – is the aim of the bundle.
- The paths in time-space are the paths of resources (solid black lines) or the paths of the uses of the resources (dashed lines).
- Resource uses are composed into bundles during a specific time (represented by the grey circles).
- A car is produced, and resources, unless materially consumed, will remain in the region.

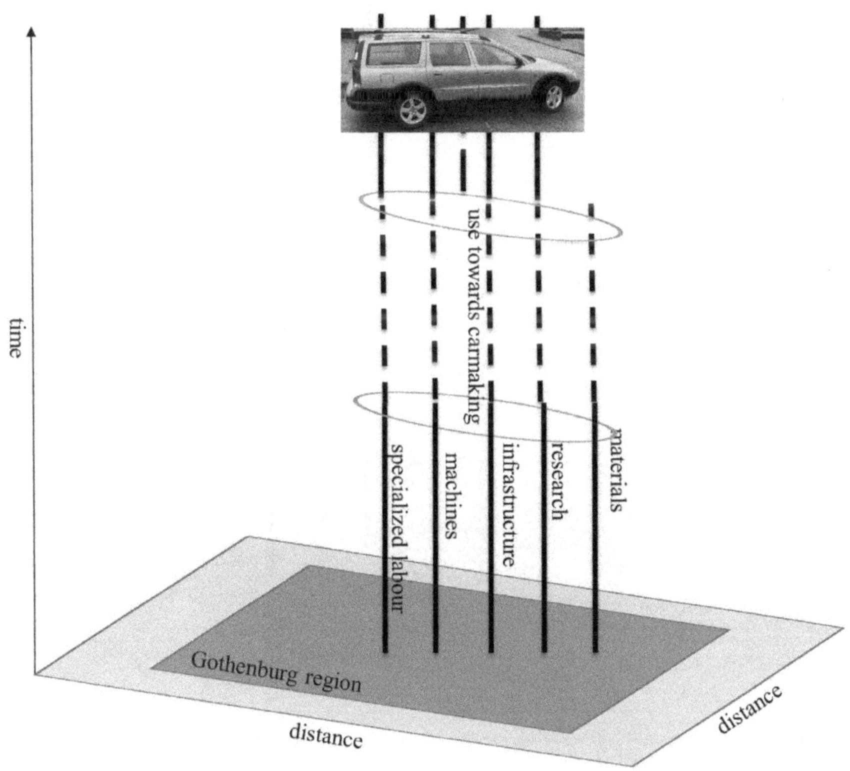

Figure 9.1 A car-making bundle in Gothenburg put in time geography graphics

Achieving the capability becomes a regional process, because the resources and uses have to be somewhere at a particular point in time. This ties Hägerstrand's time geography ideas to two concepts that we have explored before – path dependency and alternative costs – but connects them to the position of resources in time-space. Restrictions in time-space introduce regional path dependency because the possibilities of a resource to participate in other bundles are completely dependent on where in time-space the previous bundle was formed. Also, a resource cannot (at least not usually) take part in two competing bundles in time-space.

Theoretical connoisseurs find a more generalized version of exactly the same process in Figure 9.2, and we can conclude that:

- Time-space restrictions affect the bundling process and, hence, also affect where and when regional resources can be put to alternative uses.

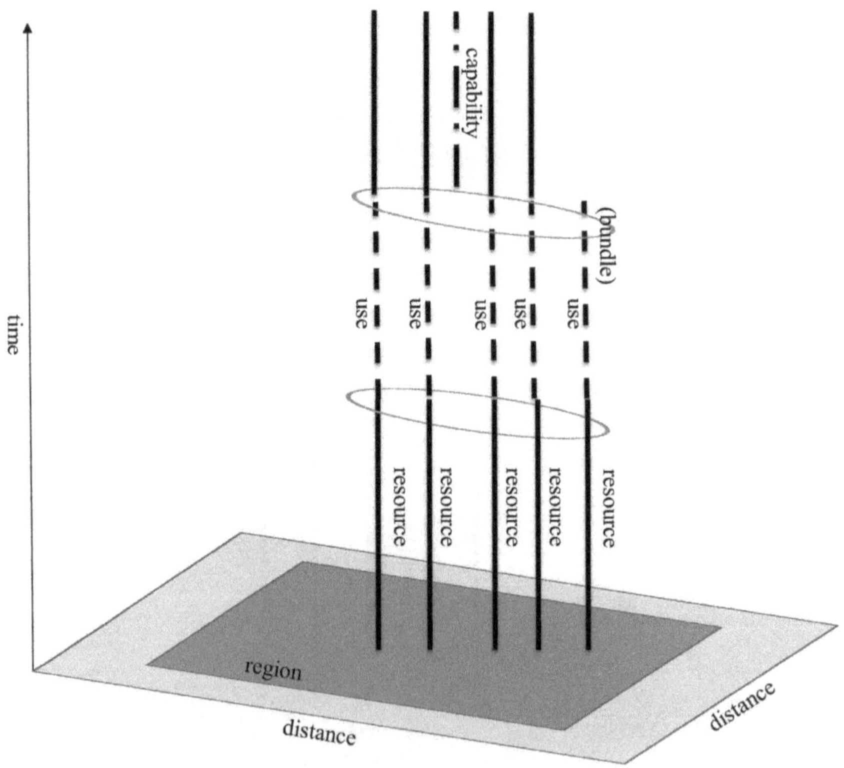

Figure 9.2 Productive bundle in time-space

- Regions without access to the resources because of the restrictions cannot achieve the capability.
- The length of the bundle (coupling restrictions) affects alternative uses, which also limits change.
- If resources are used in one bundle, they cannot normally be used in other competing bundles simultaneously.

Changed constraints

Imagine what would happen to regional economic change if the time-space constraints were to change in turn:

- Changed capability constraints: better tools of communication and transportation will change how and which resources and uses can be created and combined in bundles.
- Changed coupling constraints: the development of process technology will decrease the coupling restrictions by reducing required bundling times. One alternative for the organizing firm is to create yet another bundle (manufacture more cars), which results in economies of scale in the extension of the same capability. Qualitative change is also possible: to use idle resources in related production to develop economies of scope. Lowered coupling constraints will increase the chances of including resources in other bundles.
- Changed authority constraints: if the appropriability of a regional resource changes, the conditions to include the resource and use in the bundle change. For instance, when part of the labour force or materials are blocked from the domain where production is taking place. Power over space will directly affect the achieved capabilities of a region and its change.

Development since the second industrial revolution has significantly changed how creating and curating resources takes place within regional economies, although it has lowered capability restrictions. However, our evolutionary perspective is, so far, much too centred on the resources that the region itself can create to achieve a certain capability.

In evolutionary terms, this is probably not even the most important change that globalization of economic activities has brought about for regional economies. An obvious objection to this is that if time geography constraints change drastically and affect the portability of resource use more than the resources themselves, the bundling processes may potentially look rather different from what we have seen so far. In fact, this is exactly what has happened with globalization.

Discussion points

1. Try to sketch the corresponding picture to Figure 9.1 of a product that you value. Explain it using the concepts of time geography.
2. Are decreased time geography constraints always good? Can increased time geography constraints be justified at times?
3. In this chapter, we defined a functional region as the average workers' daily prism. What are the alternative definitions? Does it matter how a region is defined?

10

The secular change: globalization, decreased constraints and the portability of resource use

> Global production networks not only integrate firms (and parts of firms) into structures which blur traditional organizational boundaries [...], but also integrate national and local economies (or parts of such economies) in ways which have enormous implications for their economic development and well being.
>
> P. Dicken, *Global Shift*, 71

What goes on between regions and agglomerations in a globalized economy?

In earlier chapters, we developed an evolutionary perspective that discussed and took into account many of the resources, resource uses and actors involved in regional economic change, but where the relations within and between regions were kept constant. In short, what goes on within regions was seen as far more important than what goes on between them. Our approach reflected how evolutionary economic geography has developed so far, with a keen interest in how technologies in firms and industries change within regions, but with less consideration given to how links between regions change with globalization and why this is important.

This approach to regional change becomes more difficult to defend in the long run if the aim is to understand regional economic change in our time. The problem with the restricted view of regional economies – treating regional economies as "containers" little influenced of what actually happen around them – worsens with the sort of intense economic globalization that has developed since the 1980s.

One reason for the rather restricted view of regional economies and how they develop is that evolutionary economic geography (and other "container-inclined" regional approaches) did not come up with the language to consider how relations between regions change across time and with globalization, and why and how this affects the core processes of the evolutionary dynamics of regional economies. In Chapter 9, we merged the evolutionary perspective with time geography, opening up to a world of decreasing time geography constraints, which becomes important to processes of economic change in regions. Globalization has turned regional economies into something they were not before. Economic actors operate in a world characterized by deep globalization (Dicken 2015).

At the core of globalization – as one of its indicators – are the vastly increased volumes and values of global trade in manufactured goods, and lately also in services. Between 1950 and 1999, global production volumes in merchandise increased sevenfold, but export volumes increased twenty-fold and export values increased over eightyfold (based on data from World Trade Organization (WTO) n.d.a.; n.d.b.). Since 2000, the global export value of goods and services has increased threefold (data from the World Bank n.d.).

BOX 10.1 GLOBAL PRODUCTION NETWORKS

Global production networks (GPNs) is a theoretical concept that describes how the production, distribution and consumption of manufacturing goods and services take place in the global economy. GPNs are the flows by which products come into existence by a sequence of:

Inputs → Transformation (production) → Distribution → Consumption

These stages also relate to the national and global financial and institutional systems and are performed in and by different actors: transnational corporations, states, labour, consumers and civil society organizations influence the characteristics of GPNs. Core aspects of GPN analysis are: who coordinates and influences the chain? Where are different stages performed or located and why? How does geographical flexibility affect who stands to gain and where? The basic presumption of the approach is that GPNs span far more economies and products than before, but also that the complexity of the GPNs has increased enormously. GPN is one among several concepts that related literatures use to study the globalization of production. See Dicken (2015), Coe *et al.* (2004), Buckley & Ghauri (2004) and Gereffi, Humphrey & Sturgeon (2005).

To those of us interested in regional economic change, the volumes of trade are perhaps not as important as the character that this increasing trade has taken. Trade statistics tell us that not only has overall trade increased, but production and value chains have become dispersed around the globe. This means that a huge proportion of world trade is made up of components, semi-finished products and unfinished goods. Exactly how much is hard to tell, but the United Nations Conference on Trade and Development (UNCTAD) assesses that as much as one-third of world trade in 2010 was intra-firm trade (UNCTAD 2013). This type of trade reflects a far higher degree of economic complexity embedded in trade links today, compared to "just" old-style trade with raw materials on the one hand or finished manufacturing goods on the other.

Also, this trade reflects links between countries and regions that go beyond the traditional "arm's length" transactions (transactions on an open market) and mirrors far closer relationships between regions than just trade. Not only does it reflect the increased importance of foreign direct investment (FDI) but also qualitative developments in general patterns of ownership. Though FDI can be very volatile between years and is highly dependent on the general business climate, the general trend since the mid-1980s is a sharp increase in global FDI (Dicken 2015; UNCTAD 2013; 2017). The impacts are also striking in the industrialized countries. For example, in 2018, almost 40 per cent of Swedish manufacturing employees worked in foreign-owned firms, and the number of foreign-owned mid-sized manufacturing firms tripled in Sweden during 1990–2018 (Tillväxtanalys 2009; 2019). Inevitably, such ownership links must bring corporate resources that impact conditions of change in regions (Alvstam *et al.* 2019).

Ownership links, knowledge exchange and trade with input components that are on the way along a value chain towards a finished product all testify to a deeper global economic integration. In today's economy, the organizational complexity of the interregional functional links are enormous, and handling them requires extremely refined organizational routines.

The consequences of these developments are also locational. In particular, labour-intensive parts of manufacturing production have moved from high-cost economies in western Europe and North America to lower-cost economies, for example in Asia. There is still manufacturing in high-cost economies, but a shift towards high value-added and high-skill activities has certainly taken place. Again, the result is a global spatial fragmentation of value chains (where elements of production take place at different sites) and a highly intricate spatial division of labour, where regions specialize in certain stages of the production chain.

Although this is true on average, it is important to be aware that this division of labour in production is constantly and rapidly changing. For example, the days when China and India specialized in standard manufacturing alone are gone. Both countries now house regional specializations that participate in both sophisticated production and R&D at the highest global level. At the same time, other parts of the world are not as integrated in global trade and in global divisions of labour. We are still waiting for South American and African economies to capture the benefits of successful integration into the global value chains (Dicken 2015).

It would be peculiar if this secular change did not affect how resources are created, used and curated in regions. Similarly, it would be odd if globalization did not shift the emphasis of what is actually regional when it comes to the introduction of novelty, retention (path dependency) and selection in the evolutionary perspective. Conditioning this overall change are three issues: faster information-sharing between locations through information and communication technologies; cheaper, faster and safer transport across the globe; and trade liberalization.

A good way to explore the consequences of globalization on the evolutionary regional processes of economic change is to take a more detailed look at how globalization affected time-space restrictions, or rather, how reduced time-space restrictions have been a part of globalization.

We are not the first to be interested in how improvements in transportation technologies affect the prism of individuals, or how information and communication technologies affect how bundles can be created (Couclelis 2009; Neutens, Schwanen & Witlox 2011). Nor are we the first to consider how regional economies are affected by economic integration (Krugman 1991). The point is not that we are the first to consider these topics, but that the evolutionary approach to production merged with time geography allows us to develop a new angle on this process. This angle comes with interesting consequences. As we will discover, the most important impact of globalization on how regional evolutionary change happens is not at the level of resources but on how the uses of resources can be traded and exchanged across regions.

In essence, you do not need to be co-located with a resource in order to derive a use from it, at least not to the same extent as before globalization. This has fundamental consequences for evolutionary mechanisms: the introduction of novelty, retention and selection into regional economies.

Decreased constraints underpinning globalization

Improvements in transportation and communication technologies have dramatically changed the tools that we use to overcome time geography capability constraints. As a consequence, capability constraints are on average lower today than at any previous point in human history. In the geography literature, the process by which distance has come to matter less in the global economy, both as an obstacle to the transportation of goods and of information, is called time-space compression (Agnew 2001). However, the decreasing importance of distance does not mean that what goes on in places has become unimportant, as we learned from Chapters 1 and 8.

That globalization is linked to decreased capability constraints is perhaps a trivial conclusion, but consider the scale of the decrease in capability constraints and the resulting increase in portability made possible by the great technologies of transport: steamships, railways, cars, trucks and aeroplanes. The new railway line between Gothenburg and Stockholm in 1862 decreased travel time between the cities from 3 days to 12 hours. Today, the high-speed train covers the distance in less than three hours. By plane, it is about 45 minutes. Average transportation prices have plummeted too, and the standardization of shipping containers in the 1970s revolutionized goods transport.

Safety of transport has also improved. For example, the number of people killed in fatal traffic accidents in Sweden has decreased from 173 persons per 100,000 cars in 1950, to 34 per 100,000 cars in 1978, to 6 per 100,000 cars in 2018 (Trafikanalys n.d.). In 2019, the International Air Transport Association (IATA) reported 240 fatalities in world air traffic, with the total number of air travellers reaching about 4.5 billion (IATA n.d.). Notwithstanding the horrors when accidents do happen, it is virtually completely safe to fly a commercial flight. It is not only cheaper and faster to overcome capability constraints today. It is far safer too. This means that on average, improvements in the tools that we use to move economic resources and the uses of economic resources, and coordinate them in time-space, have served to drastically reduce capability constraints.

As we know from Chapter 9, higher portability influences processes of regional resource creation and use. On the one hand, importing regional resources becomes far easier. On the other hand, the risk of losing a more portable regional resource increases. Decreased capability constraints also change our very notion of what a region actually is. Above, we defined a functional region as the average workers' daily prism. If capability constraints decrease, the prism will expand. In many cases, this also means that the amount and variety of regional resources will expand as functional regions grow, expand and integrate. In Gothenburg, as in many places, the scale of this process has been massive, especially for labour. Whereas local employers' labour resource in 1900 was confined to the people that could reach the factory on foot, or in lucky circumstances by tram, the Gothenburg labour market region now covers a radius of 60 kilometres around the city's core.

It is less straightforward to analyse what has happened to coupling constraints during globalization. Coupling constraints connect strongly to the nature of production processes, which are very different for various industries and for manufacturing versus services. Nevertheless, a hint can be found in the productivity development of the manufacturing industries. Increased productivity, for example through automation, is normally linked to reduced coupling constraints, because production projects can be accomplished using shorter bundles. Since 1980, global productivity shows a clear increasing trend, even if the growth rates in advanced economies have been declining, especially after the 2009 crisis (Dieppe 2020). But what do such numbers indicate? For example, even if exact numbers differ on exactly how many hours are spent building a standard car in a factory, it remains beyond doubt that this time was reduced substantially between 1980 and 2010. Across economies, the time-space extent of bundles required for individual projects have become shorter to achieve regional capabilities. This opens up other coordination possibilities in time-space, for example that resources can be reallocated to other bundles to exploit economies of scope.

On the other hand, the level of complexity of many products has probably also increased as more resources now need to be called into a project to achieve the capability. Bundle durations have been shortened and with that the coupling constraints to individual resources, but coordinating the necessary resources into the bundle has become far more advanced and requires complex organizational routines.

Technological change also challenges the physicality of bundles in time-space and therefore the very essence of the coupling constraints in two other ways. First, technology allows people in some industries to accomplish projects without the existence of physical resource bundles. This has been noted for individual coordination in the time geography literature (Couclelis 2009), but it is also true for a wider range of economic resources. Nowadays, resource use to achieve a regional capability, at times, does not need the formation of a bundle in the traditional time geography sense at all. Sometimes a bundle has to be formed in time but not in space, such as when workers in business services accomplish a project by remote connection. In some instances, the need to form a bundle to accomplish a project has completely disappeared, for example when programming services can be split up between workers at completely different localities that do their work at different times. A production chain can be kept going around the clock. In these cases, technology has made coupling constraints obsolete.

Second, although not eliminating the need for the physical presence of maintenance staff entirely, solutions like SKF's (the Gothenburg-based rolling bearing multinational) remote conditioning services increase efficiency at times when physical bundles do have to be formed. Traditionally, the maintenance of production machinery is performed by physical inspections and repairs either at regular intervals or when machines break down (which is extremely costly to producers). Conventionally, this meant that service staff had to either travel to visit production sites or be stationed there. In both cases, time-space bundles of resource uses had to be formed, either as scheduled coordination (regular maintenance), or as a crisis event (production breakdown). SKF now offers remote diagnostic services to secure and improve functionality in customers' rotating equipment in machines. Coupling constraints are lowered, because conditioned-based maintenance lowers total demands for physical bundle formation between service people and machines. To accomplish the project of maintaining equipment (curating the regional resource), coupling constraints are down to a minimum.

Changes in the authority constraints that hamper the creation, use and curation of regional resources makes globalization a much broader story than being solely about technological change. On average, there are reasons to argue that these authority constraints have also decreased. But, as we know from research in economic geography and international business, they still play an important role when it comes to how resources can be bundled in time-space and why bundles look so different across countries and regions.

The most obvious change in authority constraints in our time, which affect resource mobility, are institutional changes at the macro level, globally or between individual countries, that decrease authority constraints. The General Agreement on Tariffs and Trade (GATT)/WTO has made global trade cheaper and easier. The WTO estimates that from average tariff levels among industrial countries of between 20 and 30 per cent after the Second World War, average global tariffs were down to 11 per cent in 1996 and 9 per cent in 2019 (WTO n.d.b). In manufacturing, average tariffs are even lower. This is a formidable change. FDI policies have been relaxed worldwide too, and different integration initiatives are progressing (Buckley, Enderwick & Cross 2018). Levels of FDI restrictions, such as regulations regarding limits to ownership, have decreased drastically among the Organisation for Economic Co-operation and Development countries between 1980 and 2000 (Golub 2003). One source of such achievements is the integration of the single European market, which guarantees free movement of goods, capital, services and labour between the member states in the EU and associated countries.

In sum, a vast range of institutional reforms striving for economic integration have made it easier for many regions to build, use, import and export their regional resources. Far lower authority constraints for economic resources during globalization have changed when and where economic resources can be used across the globe and at what cost. For example, many high-income countries in the EU, including Sweden, have benefitted from work-related in-migration of productive workers from new member states in the eastern part of the EU to support their regional economies. By partly changing the appropriability of resources, this inflow of workers has created important additions to regional resources. In these examples, reduced authority constraints have made it more feasible to compose productive bundles in regions and to achieve a capability. In some cases, this "import" of resources has proven to be absolutely necessary for regional economies to sustain certain capabilities, for example in the agriculture and tourism sectors.

Although the GATT/WTO and EU are maybe the most obvious examples of how traditional domains that limit creation and use of regional resources can be expanded, the movement towards lower authority constraints and increased resource portability is no natural law. Authority constraints can change very quickly. The drastic measures that governments around the world took to prevent the spread of Covid-19 in 2020 is a good example of this. Suddenly, as cross-border travel was largely banned, a completely new set of time-space domains were established for economic resources, primarily labour. Also, there are still many parts of the world where the creation of economic productive resources are hampered by severe time-space constraints. But all in all, the domains that matter to regional economic change look very different today compared to 40 years ago.

Yet, these changes also carry consequences for the regions that end up on the resource "exporting" side. For example, within the EU, notwithstanding the overall positive effects of general mobility, some regional governments will, quite understandably, worry about the out-migration of skilled and young workers. Also, if the export of regional fixed capital means that resources themselves are dismantled and moved to participate in projects in other regions, it will prove difficult to reverse the process.

Given this evidence, it is curious to think that the overall decreases of time geography constraints and the changes in relationships between regions that it involves does not change the introduction of novelty, retention and selection processes within regional economies. Even 20 years ago, the time-space-related possibilities that regions had to create, build and curate their resources looked very different. Time geography has opened some interesting avenues to investigate this issue further.

But lower constraints on how regional resources are created, used and curated are not the most important changes that globalization has brought to the introduction of novelty, retention and selection processes in regional economies. The most significant change can be traced to the level of resource use, and how globalization is about increasing the portability of resource use without moving the resources themselves. This factor has really changed things.

Globalization, portability of resource uses and regional economic change

The higher portability of uses derived from regional resources in regions across the globe underpins much of the geographically dispersed, flexible and lean production methods that many firms apply today (Dicken 2015). This higher portability of resource use is achieved by lower time geography constraints. Lower capability, coupling and authority constraints have changed the need for regions to actually create resources themselves in order to be able to develop capabilities. The resulting trade with uses derived from resources across the world, coordinated into projects by end producers, marks the real productive essence of globalization.

A fine and complex division of labour between firms, and regions, is a prerequisite for keeping all the extremely advanced capacities in today's economy running. Very few firms, or even regions, could uphold such a wide repertoire of capabilities without importing uses derived from resources in other regions. In the globalized economy, regions develop specializations based on the competitive advantages of their resources, agglomerations and routines, and then export the uses derived from the regional resources as inputs along international production networks. This is the growing potential for regions to export the uses derived from their regional resources. These uses could be services in the form of specific product of labour or input components along value chains, and they participate in further bundling processes that take place in other regions.

To understand how the increased portability of resource uses has allowed the trade in input components to explode into the spatially fragmented, but functionally linked, global production networks (Coe *et al.* 2004) or global factories (Buckley, Enderwick & Cross 2018), we need to add two aspects to our evolutionary perspective on production. First, how decreased coupling constraints have been complemented by the fact that information and services can be traded in new ways. Second, how outsourcing and offshoring have become far easier.

Because information can be shared in radically new ways through globalization, the time geography's traditional conditioning of projects on time-space coordination has partially changed. The internet, video meetings, remote process control and remote monitoring are just some of the technologies making distance and possibly place less important. This means that resources can be located in one region, but the uses of those resources can be bundled in another region. Achieving the final capability does not require complete coordination in time-space of uses, and certainly not of resources. This alters where regional resources can be located in order to participate in a bundle. In some industries, this has even made the formation of production bundles in space less important and allowed for bundles in which resources with physical presence in space is combined with a "virtual" presence.

A useful way to think about this change is to consider the filter effects that accompany different information technologies (Daft & Lengel 1986; Törnqvist 1997). In an information exchange, as when two people talk, much more information is filtered if they talk by telephone than if they meet. Facial expressions, small sounds, gestures; all this disappears over the phone. With new communication technologies, the filter effects have changed rapidly. Traditionally, geographers would, for example, assume that a Gothenburg firm using skill resources for advanced programming in India would face greater obstacles than having the programming resource present in Gothenburg. Nowadays, we can be far less sure that is the case. Thanks to modern technology, advanced programming staff in India can be readily used in a Gothenburg production bundle.

This is where the evolutionary approach meets contemporary ideas about outsourcing. In some cases of outsourcing, proximity is still required. In these cases, the end-producing firm may outsource business service functions to consultants and invite them to work at the end producer's physical location or outsource to another firm in the region. From a regional point of view this makes little difference; it allows for firm specialization but where outsourced uses are still derived from the same regional resource of the local pool of skilled labour. Such outsourcing has more to do with demands for flexibility and organizational ideas than with changing time-space restrictions.

If firms choose to outsource and relocate (offshore) production, things take a radically different turn. Let us use offshoring as a very general term, as something happening when firms locate production, or a part of the production, outside the original region. Although many management and firm routine implications could be drawn from the distinction between offshoring under conditions of outsourcing (letting other firms manage part of the production in another region and/or country) or offshoring as an internal firm process (by starting a sister company in another country under the same ownership) (Buckley, Enderwick & Cross 2018), this is of less importance to our particular discussion. The regional consequences are almost the same.

Spatial fragmentation of production, outsourcing and offshoring all point to the same phenomenon: global production networks and global factories require trade with uses that are derived from regional resources in other regions, and this trade has become far more important over time.

Take the example with the programmer in India working for the Gothenburg firm. The Gothenburg firm directly derives uses from a resource in another region to achieve a bundle and a regional capability in Gothenburg, namely to develop a new computer program. Or take the auto industry in Gothenburg, which buys important components for its cars from German suppliers instead of making the components themselves. It imports a resource use (producing the component) that it bundles to achieve the regional capability of car manufacture.

The regional import of components for a final product means that resource use is imported (either as intra-firm trade or business-to-business trade) to developing a capability (to make the final product). In many cases today, developing a regional capability includes importing uses derived from resources of other regions and integrating them with regionally derived uses to achieve the desired capacity. Decreased time-space restrictions allow for extensive trade in resource uses, where regional capabilities are achieved through the combined bundling of uses derived from regional resources with those that are derived from resources located in other regions, sometimes across the world.

Let us try to include this in our evolutionary perspective, where we move from regional resources to regional capabilities (Figure 10.1). On the third level of our perspective, we add imported uses from other regions.

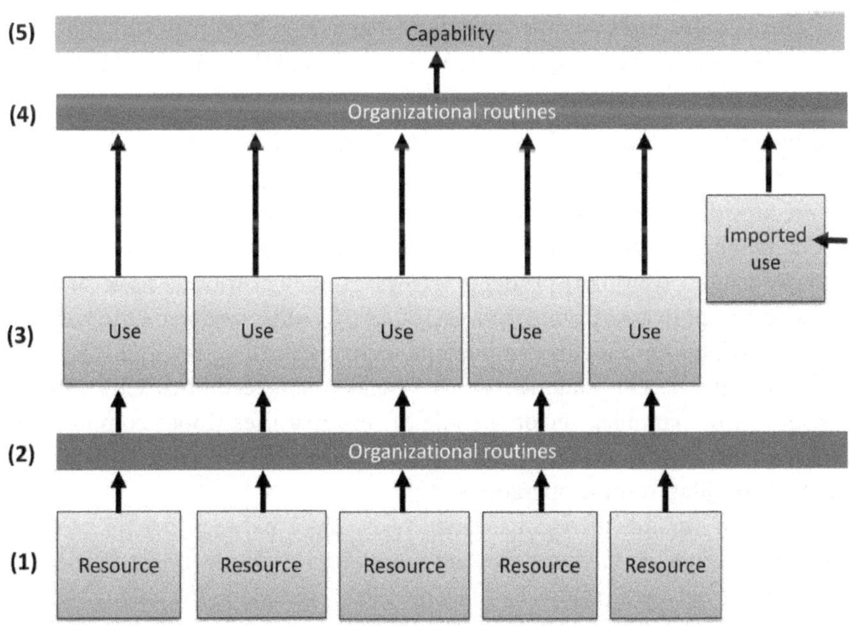

Figure 10.1 The evolutionary perspective allowing for import of uses derived from resources in other regions

In sum, the evolutionary productive systems of regions are no longer containers. What goes on between regions may be as important to regional economic change as the recombination processes going on within regions. This changes the fundamentals of the introduction of novelty, retention and selection in ways that include the following:

- Novelty: reduced time geography constraints have increased opportunities for achieving new bundles consisting of uses derived from resources based within the region, with uses derived from resources based outside the region. The balance between intra- and extra-regional resources varies across industries, firms and regions.
- Retention: reduced time geography constraints make it, in principle, easier to escape regional path dependency. However, in order to capitalize on uses from resources based in other regions, organizational routines and complementary regional services need to be in place. Not all regions possess these routines.
- Selection: reduced time geography constraints have turned selection pressures from the regional and national level to the global level. However, globalization has also meant that regions can compete on the basis of providing particular exportable uses based on their regional resources rather than competing on the resulting capability (the end product). In parallel, many firms survive selection pressures because they take advantage of this opportunity to purchase uses based on resources in other regions and then rebundling them.

Use imports, and cars and trucks for the last time!

To see how this works in real life, we revisit the production of cars and trucks in Gothenburg. We have made the theoretical point that just as regions import and export end (finished) products (the cars), they also trade uses, such as skills or components, derived from resources in other regions. One version of this is when the trade of components happens within a firm but between different regions. For example, Volvo Trucks' main facility in Gothenburg engages in the complex regional trade of resource uses (input components and services) between its factories in Sweden and across the world. This is part of their everyday, routine operations.

A second version of regional trade takes place between firms but with components that are further down the value chain from the finished product. This is trade between regions and between firms but along the value chain of a product. For example, in general, cars consist of thousands of components, many of which are not made by the end manufacturers, the "car makers", themselves (Teknikens värld n.d.). Because of the pervasiveness of outsourcing, offshoring and the benefits of firm specialization, production of many manufacturing products, maybe even most, share this feature. In complex industries, suppliers are often core actors when it comes to the technical development of advanced products.

In reality, Gothenburg imports car components and services of a great variety in technological intensity to assemble into the cars built in Gothenburg. Although subcontractor mappings are not easy to come by, because they are strategic business secrets, recent numbers suggest that about two-thirds of components in a modern car are produced by other suppliers than the brand firm, some of them from the same region, some not (Teknikens värld n.d.). The auto industry's capability to produce cars actually draws on a complex and distributed set of subcontractors. This means that the capability to build a car in Gothenburg is predicated on a complex interplay between uses derived from resources in Gothenburg and imported uses that draw from resources in other regions. Brand firms becomes masters at coordinating this; they become extraordinarily good at composing the bundle that accomplishes the capability. In 2008, this meant that Volvo Cars coordinated the inputs of 500 subcontractors delivering directly to Volvo Cars. Twenty per cent of these were Swedish (SvD 2008).

The overall scale of these regional imports of components, which are material representatives of uses delivered into a region to help it achieve a regional capability, is immense. In Sweden alone, tens of thousands of people across the country work in firms that supply components to the car industry, both as manufactured components and as design services. The big players among the suppliers, such as Bosch, Autoliv and Trelleborg, are huge firms in themselves, with their own resource and routines. The logistical challenges of this spatial fragmentation of work are enormous. In Gothenburg, inputs from suppliers have to arrive at the gates of the factory in 15-minute time windows. In modern economies, firms invest huge resources into developing their organizational routines to accommodate and overcome time-space coordination problems.

Although car manufacture is one of the dominant categories of production in Gothenburg, it is of course completely untrue that Gothenburg can produce a car by itself. Because the modern automobile industry is complex, it is obvious that resources located within one region and the uses derived from them are not sufficient to achieve the regional capability of building a car. Because of this, some uses need to be derived from resources in other regions and imported to Gothenburg if the region is to build a car that can compete on the world market and survive selection.

Gothenburg can achieve the rare capability of car making by producing some of the components and by being skilled in assembly, but foremost this is achieved by being really skilled at employing routines to organize the bundle of resource uses required to make a car.

As a consequence, to achieve the capability of making a complex product, a region does not need to create all the resources needed to derive the uses needed. In many cases, the region is better off importing the right uses. Figure 10.2 includes the import of resource uses in the model about car making, as an addition to level 3.

Cars are among the more complex products in the economy that require end producers capable of coordinating vast volumes of exported and imported resource uses. Yet, on a smaller scale, the same kind of reasoning is valid for many, if not most, manufacturing products.

Also, cars are not the most complex products that require the extensive regional imports of resource uses. A modern Airbus aircraft is built all over Europe, and the firm's final assembly lines can be found in Toulouse and Hamburg. Getting the components to the site is an amazingly complex operation, involving enormous custom-designed BelugaXT airlifters, specially commissioned ships, barges and trucks, as well as more conventional modes of transport. This is merely the import of uses that goes into the production of the Airbus. Uses are derived from resources all over Europe and are imported into Toulouse or Hamburg.

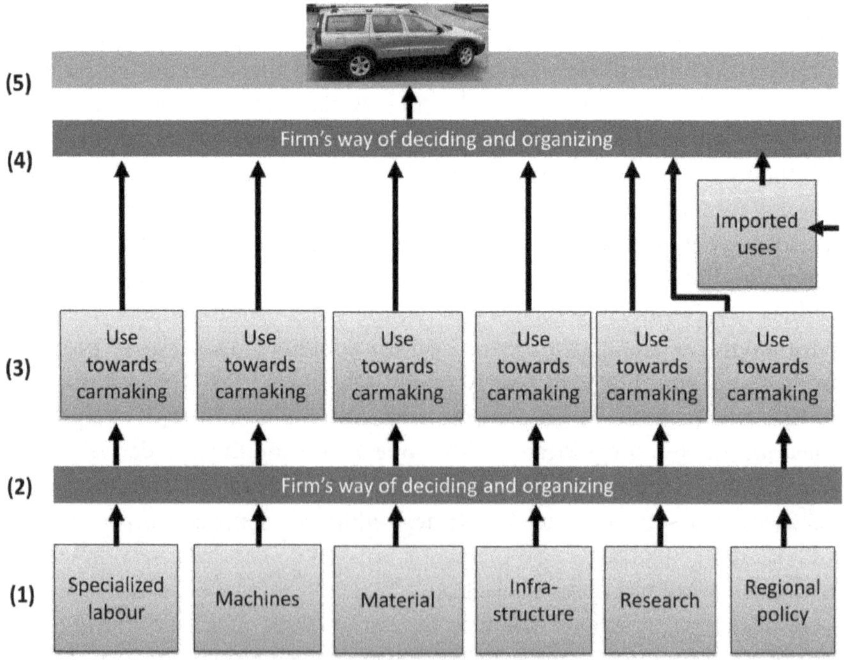

Figure 10.2 Car production allowing for the import of uses derived from resources in other regions

This also adds cumulative complexity to our evolutionary perspective. In the real economy, products are built by repeated sequences of levels 1–5 of our evolutionary perspective, where production is intertwined in complex ways. In that sense, products that are inputs along the value chain of certain finished goods can all be seen as delivering uses to that finished good, because these products are of no use to end costumers. Few airlines will have much use of a wing section alone, regardless of how sophisticated this is. It only makes sense as part of a bundle of resource uses in achieving the final capability in Toulouse and Hamburg: an airliner.

Globalization has changed the way that evolutionary economic change takes place in regions, and its core reasons are the decreases in time geography constraints. During the course of history, and especially during the twentieth century, the ways in which regions create, use and curate resources, and the need to do so to achieve regional capabilities, have changed tremendously. This means that regional resources and uses play a different role today in economic development than they used to do: it is still largely about Schumpeter's *neue Kombinationen* (new combinations) but on a spatial scale that Schumpeter could hardly foresee. At the end of the day, or rather, where the process is at now, lower capability, coupling and authority constraints have changed the need for regions to create resources themselves to develop productive capabilities.

Finally, in the time geography graphics, economic globalization is described in Figure 10.3. Compare it to Figure 9.2. To derive uses for a bundle, resources in three different regions are used. Because of higher portability through globalization, specific resource uses are exported from regions 1 and 3, and used in the bundling in region 2, to achieve a regional capability. This is exactly what happens with cars. And in many cases, this means that the resources themselves, such as skills, remain in their original regions, even though their uses are exported to be bundled into an final product in another region.

Export of resource use

Finally, we need to turn the arguments about imports of resource uses around. Just as decreasing time geography constraints have made the import of uses derived from resources in other regions far easier, this has also facilitated the export of uses from regional resources. And just as this has meant that regions do not need to develop all the resources they need to achieve a regional capability themselves, it also means that regions can easily export uses for bundles and the achievement of regional capabilities in other regions.

But what does all this mean in terms of the evolutionary argument about regional change and for regional policy?

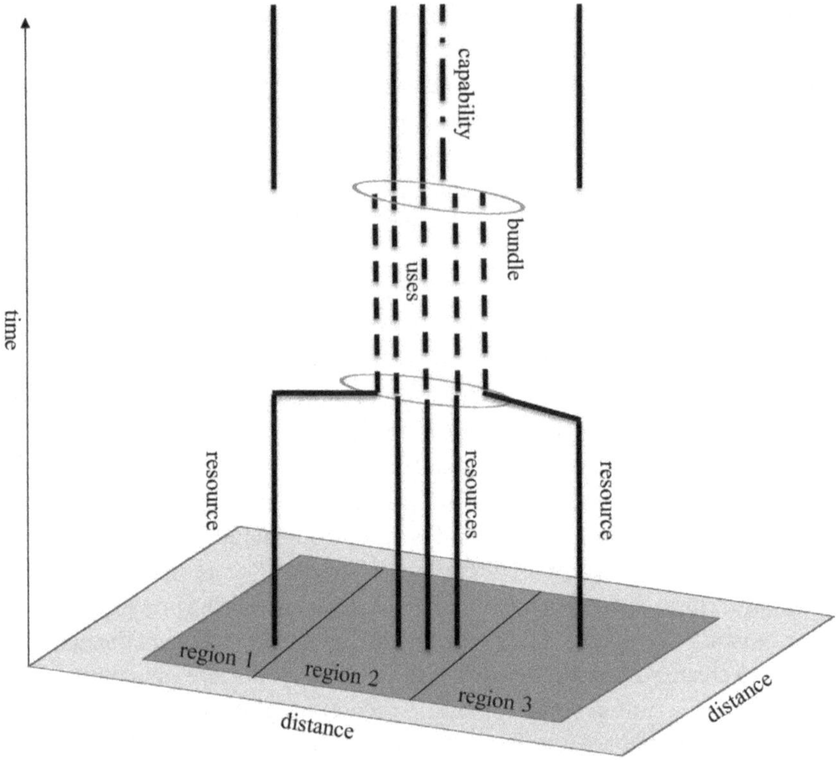

Figure 10.3 Globalization dressed as time geography

Discussion points

1. How important are organizational routines in order to orchestrate resource uses into capabilities? Does the importance differ depending on the complexity of the production?
2. When does the price of deriving a use from a regional resource become too high? Try to think of an example when a resource use transforms from being locally derived to being imported. Why did this change take place? What were the effects?
3. (Final grand challenge!) Pick a product produced in your region and try to pinpoint some of the resources needed to produce it, and which specific resource uses are derived to produce the product. On average, how many of the resources are from your region? Are they organizational, hybrid or regional? Which resource uses are imported? How has this changed across time? Try to draw a similar picture to the one above (Figure 10.3).

11

Conclusions

Globalization fundamentally changed how the core processes of evolutionary economic geography – the introduction of novelty, retention and selection in regional economies – work. In fact, one could argue that decreased time geography constraints – lower capability, coupling and authority constraints – together with how regional actors react to and make use of them, *are* globalization. Therefore, economic change, and the way in which it is a spatial phenomenon, looks very different today than it did 100, 50 or even 30 years ago.

In essence and on average, this globalization has been a good thing. Increased portability of resource uses creates problems for some regions, where the closing down of pathways has led to lock-in and organizational routines have not been able to adapt, but it creates opportunities for others that skilfully create, use and curate their regional resources. It is the global division of labour and the thousands of resource specializations around the world that have allowed the world economy to produce such endless economic variety in our time.

So far, and for many reasons, evolutionary economic geographers have been overwhelmingly concerned with what goes on among actors and technologies within regions, and how regional processes affect the introduction of novelty, retention and selection. But in a globalized economy, one with decreasing time geography constraints, it becomes increasingly difficult to understand economic change in regions without explicitly taking into account what goes on between regions. How can you explain economic change in Gothenburg or Borås, or even relevant fractions of it, without taking globalization into account as well? It is not that evolutionary economic geographers never had such thoughts, but the traditional evolutionary view was more focused on explaining how regions were still important in a globalized world, rather than investigating how regional and global aspects meet to explain evolutionary economic change. In this book, time geography has provided some tools to make the global and the regional meet in a productionist evolutionary perspective on regional economic change.

In a globalized economy, a region does not need to possess all the regional resources and locally draw the uses needed to achieve a productive capability. This insight is not new, but by combining time geography with the evolutionary view on regional economies, we have tried to make it obvious how this actually happens and how it links to regional economic change. But it also links directly to regional specialization. What can and should regional economies actually specialize in today?

In a globalized economy, regions normally need to possess some localized resources, and then spend a lot of effort on coordinating the productive bundle that achieves a capability, including imported resource uses from other regions. This is so, because the time geography restrictions that used to hinder trade in derived resource uses have partially eroded. This means that for many firms, the challenge is not only to master the coordination of regional resources and their use but to master and sustain the core ones, as well as supporting the firm routines that allows the firm to coordinate local and extra-local uses into a bundle that achieves a regional capability. Gothenburg thrives from its many brand firms in various industries, but this does not mean that it houses all the regional resources needed to sustain its regional capabilities.

The increased export of resource uses with globalization creates opportunities for more peripheral regions too, at least in principle. To participate in bundles, resources do not have to be coordinated in space to the extent that they used to be. This means that resources can stay in their original regions to a greater extent than before. Consequently, the problem of many peripheral and small regions, primarily the regional losers in the globalization process (at least so far), is not the geography of resource use any more. Resource uses can be exported, and imported too. Instead, the problem is the creation and curation of resources with a high-enough degree of specificity in those places. The creation of resources, at least man-made ones, is expensive. Many smaller regions cannot afford to do so. Curating the resources is also more difficult, because scale efficiencies cannot be as easily reached (e.g. in training programmes), and many of the actors that engage in resource curation are simply not present in these kinds of regions. To some extent, problems in resource creation and curation can be mediated by regional policies. Economic change, also in the location of economic activities, is a natural and integral part of an evolving market economy. In such a world, the solution becomes not to stall change but to compensate the people and regions that without any fault of their own, but rather by the logics of economic evolution, suffer from change.

Policy as a regional resource

So, at the end of the day, what is the role of regional economic policy in all this?

The impacts and importance of regional policy – meaning the initiatives that regional policy-makers, politicians and their organizations take to promote productive regional change – can be fruitfully divided into three domains according to the evolutionary view: resource creation, resource curation and capability branching. These domains are productionist, which means that they do not consider other fields where regional policy also has important functions, such as in ensuring that markets work properly or in implementing targeted policy.

Resource creation and use

In Chapter 6, we concluded that some regional resources are created by regional policy and the actors that regional policy govern directly. Yet, other regional resources are created through initiatives from regional policy and policy-makers. Two of the most important areas are education and regional infrastructure. The arguments for regional policy taking a lead role in the creation of a skilled labour force is straightforward, and builds on traditional economic concerns. If left to the market, there is a risk of underinvestment in some dimensions of resource creation. Therefore, governments (regional and national) need to take active roles here.

Chapter 5 even argued that regional policy is (or can be) a regional resource in itself. This is because regional policy at times works with mundane initiatives and processes that are nevertheless important to regional resource creation and use. Many of these initiatives are perhaps not the policies that end up in brochures or in newspaper headlines, but they are policies about land allocation for production, speed limits on local roads, production permits and a long list of other factors that affect the everyday creation and use of economic resources. For example, the Confederation of Swedish Enterprise ranks the "local business climate" in Swedish municipalities every year. In 2020, Gothenburg was ranked 189th among 290 municipalities, and Borås 99th. Even if such rankings cause concern, they still testify to the importance that firms, and firm confederations, attach to regional policy. In that sense, regional policy is clearly a resource that delivers some of the everyday uses needed to achieve regional capabilities.

Resource curation

Chapter 6 also investigated the importance of resource curation. Although some branches of policy – especially those concerned with regional cluster development – are engaged in telling the world about the resources and advantages of their particular region, one could argue that the maintenance side of resources has received much less attention.

Curation of labour is a particular concern. Traditionally, policy (at national and regional levels) focuses on education and vocational training for young people, whereas further education has only been on the policy agenda in a pervasive way over the last couple of years. As technical change accelerates, the skills that are required among the regional labour force change too. The human capital in a region becomes a resource that has to be maintained and taken care of during its lifetime to stay productive. Because we are still locked into our second industrial revolution views about what a job and an education should be, and when and how an education should be offered to people, most regions have not yet developed a sustainable approach to dealing with resource curation for human skills. This is therefore a huge challenge, which requires both functional and cognitive policy change.

Capability branching: smart specialization

The EU's economic policy framework for smart specialization aims to help regions develop "smart specialization strategies" as a way to make regional policy initiatives and projects more coherent and better linked to present regional resources and strengths (EU n.d.c). Smart specialization is understood as a general approach to regional change, rather than as a framework with a certain set of policies. Although smart specialization is mainly a concept associated with the EU, the underlying ideas are representative of shifts in regional policy-making that have also occurred elsewhere outside the Union.

The smart specialization approach is basically not productionist, it is more about innovation (Chapter 2). Yet, it implicitly assumes that innovation will have outcomes in terms of regional productive change "to boost growth and jobs in Europe" (EU n.d.d). In that sense, it is also productionist:

> A S3 [Smart specialization Strategy] should prioritise domains, areas and economic activities where regions or countries have a competitive advantage or have the potential to generate knowledge-driven growth and to bring about the economic transformation needed to tackle the major and most urgent challenges for the society and the natural and

> built environment. The number and nature of these priorities will vary from region to region. Note however, that although a first set of priorities should be identified when the S3 is designed, they can be changed or modified when new information/developments make it advisable.
> (EU n.d.e)

As you might have already noticed, smart specialization shares many of its assumptions and its approach with evolutionary economic geography. Smart specialization also struggles with exactly the same issues as we have encountered throughout this book: the balance between the need of incremental and radical change, between specialization and variety and between creation and destruction as outcomes of economic change.

But there is one particular issue that is highlighted by smart specialization that we have not yet mentioned: regional-related diversification (Balland *et al.* 2019). In Chapter 1, a European Commission statement was cited: "The most promising way for a region to promote its knowledge-based growth is to diversify into technologies, products and services that are closely related to existing dominant technologies and the regional skills base" (European Commission 2014).

Up to now, we have walked through quite an elaborate theory of what constitutes "closely related", why that is important and the potential risks involved in "related" diversification. The evolutionary approach allows us to relate smart specialization to a greater context of regional change, using the same terminology.

It is debatable whether the main role of regional policy should be to support and stimulate incremental productive change in regions, radical change or no particular type of change (i.e. engage more in the creation and curation of very general resources). It is probable that the answer depends on the situation. Normally, the financial resources to implement regional policy are limited, and most of the time it can at best support path-based incremental change, and in particular resource curation.

However, if all or most realistic development paths in a region come to a close, policy needs to promote radical regional change. It is costly and risky, but in situations of true lock-in, it is hard to conceive of other strategies.

Next steps

There are a couple of other pertinent issues that the discussions in this book have not delved into too deeply, which are interesting potential fields for further research.

First, according to the evolutionary view presented in this book, the goal of regional diversification seems almost automatic and omnipresent, given the presence of resources and/or prospects to import resources. But economic diversification is obviously something performed by those who have the agency to change things. So, on the one hand, we could, and probably should, go deeper into the issue of the driving forces of regional diversification. Why do entrepreneurs and firms take diversification decisions in the first place? By Schumpeterian evolutionary logics, a main motivation for diversification would mainly be to get ahead of selection pressures in the market. To stay in business and capture rents, entrepreneurs and firms in regions take diversification decisions. Such processes seem to be pervasive features of the capitalist economy. Given this, a lot of evolutionary research has actually concentrated on why regional diversification does not take place: because of different kinds of lock-ins for instance. Yet, of course, diversification in terms of reaching new capabilities requires deliberate action or, using a more modern term, "agency". Evolutionary economic geography and entrepreneurship research have a lot to gain from more interaction on this issue (Henning & McKelvey 2020).

Second, a foundational economic idea which is not only to be found in Schumpeterian economics, is that creative destruction takes place as a resource transfer process from old and obsolete to new and growing activities. An important issue, also for regional policy, becomes how the evolutionary view adds to the traditional resource transfer idea in economics.

A provisional answer could be that the traditional resource transfer idea is problematic, because it somehow assumes that resources can actually be transferred and be of productive use in growing activities and contributing to new capabilities. However, because resources are to different degrees specific, some resources cannot. This notion is elegantly captured in the regional path dependency literature. It was also discussed by the Swedish economist Eric Dahmén, who talked of the positive and negative sides of economic transformation (Dahmén 1984; 1988). Sometimes, economic change is just more destructive than creative. The entire trick is then to curate resources so that their uses become attractive to new combinations (reduce specificity of the resource) or to build completely new resources. Either strategy is easier said than done. Creative destruction is a great theoretical idea, but it is of little help to workers laid off in shipbuilding to tell them that they are just part of the greater scheme of economic change. They need help to stay relevant in turbulent times of economic change, and that help is an important part of legitimizing economic change itself.

Curating resources can be a way to improve economic performance, but it is also a way to make established regional resources, such as labour, participate in regional change. Regional economic change needs to be legitimate. If it is not, many will be more interested in economic revolution than evolution.

References

Agnew, J. 2001. "The new global economy: time-space compression, geopolitics, and global uneven development". *Journal of World-Systems Research* 7(2): 133–54.

Alvstam, C.-G, M. Henning, I. Ivarsson, R. Nakamura & R. Yakob 2019. Strategiskt förnyelsearbete inom svensk industri. VINNOVA RAPPORT VR 2020:07.

Amin, A. 2003. "Industrial districts". In E. Sheppard & T. Barnes (eds), *A Companion to Economic Geography*. Oxford: Blackwell.

Asheim, B. 2000. "Industrial districts: the contributions of Marshall and beyond". In G. Clark, M. Feldman & M. Gertler (eds), *The Oxford Handbook of Economic Geography*, 413–31. Oxford: Oxford University Press.

Balland, P., R. Boschma, J. Crespo & D. Rigby 2019. "Smart specialization policy in the European Union: relatedness, knowledge complexity and regional diversification". *Regional Studies* 53(9): 1252–68.

Barney, J. 1991. "Firm resources and sustained competitive advantage". *Journal of Management* 17: 99–120.

Bathelt, H. & J. Glückler 2003. "Toward a relational economic geography". *Journal of Economic Geography* 3(2): 117–44.

Berger, T., K. Enflo & M. Henning 2012. "Geographical location and urbanization of the Swedish manufacturing industry, 1900–1960: evidence from a new database". *Scandinavian Economic History Review* 60(3): 290–308.

Boschma, R. 1997. "New industries and windows of locational opportunity: a long-term analysis of Belgium". *Erdkunde*: 12–22.

Boschma, R. 2004. "Competitiveness of regions from an evolutionary perspective". *Regional Studies* 38(9): 1001–14.

Boschma, R. 2005. "Proximity and innovation: a critical assessment". *Regional studies* 39(1): 61–74.

Boschma, R., P. Balland & D. Kogler 2015. "Relatedness and technological change in cities: the rise and fall of technological knowledge in US metropolitan areas from 1981 to 2010". *Industrial and Corporate Change* 24(1): 223–50.

Boschma, R. & K. Frenken 2006. "Why is economic geography not an evolutionary science? Towards an evolutionary economic geography". *Journal of Economic Geography* 6(3): 273–302.

Boschma, R. & K. Frenken 2009. "Some notes on institutions in evolutionary economic geography". *Economic Geography* 85(2): 151–8.

Boschma, R. & K. Frenken 2011. "The emerging empirics of evolutionary economic geography". *Journal of Economic Geography* 11(2): 295–307.

Boschma, R. & S. Iammarino 2009. "Related variety, trade linkages, and regional growth in Italy". *Economic Geography* 85(3): 289–311.

Boschma, R. & R. Martin (eds) 2010. *The Handbook of Evolutionary Economic Geography*. Cheltenham: Edward Elgar.

Boschma, R., A. Minondo & M. Navarro 2013. "The emergence of new industries at the regional level in Spain: a proximity approach based on product relatedness". *Economic Geography* 89(1): 29–51.

Bowin, J. (ed.) 2011. *Kompetensförsörjning: Från strategi till resultat*. Stockholm: SIS Förlag.

Brauer, M. & T. Laamanen 2014. "Workforce downsizing and firm performance: an organizational routine perspective". *Journal of Management Studies* 51(8): 1311–33.

Buckley, P., P. Enderwick & A. Cross (eds) 2018. *International Business*. Oxford: Oxford University Press.

Buckley, P. & P. Ghauri 2004. "Globalisation, economic geography and the strategy of multinational enterprises". *Journal of International Business Studies* 35(2): 81–98.

Cantwell, J. & R. Mudambi 2011. "Physical attraction and the geography of knowledge sourcing in multinational enterprises". *Global Strategy Journal* 1(3/4): 206–32.

Castaldi, C., K. Frenken & B. Los 2015. "Related variety, unrelated variety and technological breakthroughs: an analysis of US state-level patenting". *Regional Studies* 49(5): 767–81.

Coe, N., M. Hess, H. Yeung, P. Dicken & J. Henderson 2004. "'Globalizing' regional development: a global production networks perspective". *Transactions of the Institute of British Geographers* 29(4): 468–84.

Content, J. & K. Frenken 2016. "Related variety and economic development: a literature review". *European Planning Studies* 24(12): 2097–112.

Couclelis, H. 2009. "Rethinking time geography in the information age". *Environment and Planning A* 41(7): 1556–75.

Daft, R. & R. Lengel 1986. "Organizational information requirements, media richness and structural design". *Management Science* 32(5): 554–71.

Dahmén, E. 1980. "Hur studera industriell utveckling?" In E. Dahmén & G. Eliasson (eds), *Industriell utveckling i Sverige: Teori och verklighet under ett sekel*. Stockholm: IUI.

Dahmén, E. 1984. "Schumpeterian dynamics: some methodological notes". *Journal of Economic Behavior & Organization* 5(1): 25–34.

Dahmén, E. 1988. "'Development blocks' in industrial economics". *Scandinavian Economic History Review* 36(1): 3–14.

David, P. 1985. "Clio and the economics of QWERTY". *American Economic Review* 75(2): 332–7.

Delgado, M., M. Porter & S. Stern 2014. "Clusters, convergence, and economic performance". *Research Policy* 43(10): 1785–99.

Dicken, P. 2015. *Global Shift*. London: Sage.

Dieppe, A. (ed.) 2020. *Global Productivity: Trends, Drivers, and Policies*. Washington, DC: World Bank.

Dunning, J. 1998. "Globalization and the new geography of foreign direct investment". *Oxford Development Studies* 26(1): 47–69.

Duranton, G. & D. Puga 2001. "Nursery cities: urban diversity, process innovation, and the life cycle of products". *American Economic Review* 91(5): 1454–77.

Economist 2012. "A sense of place". *The Economist* 405 (8808): 99–201.

Ellegård, K. & U. Svedin 2012. "Torsten Hägerstrand's time-geography as the cradle of the activity approach in transport geography". *Journal of Transport Geography* 23: 17–25.

Ellison, G. & E. Glaeser 1997. "Geographic concentration in US manufacturing industries: a dartboard approach". *Journal of Political Economy* 105(5): 889–927.

Enflo, K. & M. Henning 2016. "The development of economic growth and inequality among the Swedish regions 1860–2010: evidence from regional national accounts". In J. Ljungberg (ed.), *Structural Analysis and the Process of Economic Development: Essays in Memory of Lennart Schön*, 127–48. Abingdon: Routledge.

Eriksson, R., E. Hane-Weijman & M. Henning 2018. "Sectoral and geographical mobility of workers after large establishment cutbacks or closures". *Environment and Planning A: Economy and Space* 50(5): 1071–91.

Eriksson, R., M. Henning & A. Otto 2016. "Industrial and geographical mobility of workers during industry decline: the Swedish and German shipbuilding industries 1970–2000". *Geoforum* 75: 87–98.

Eriksson, R., U. Lindgren & G. Malmberg 2008. "Agglomeration mobility: effects of localisation, urbanisation, and scale on job changes". *Environment and Planning A* 40(10): 2419–34.

Essletzbichler, J. 2015. "Relatedness, industrial branching and technological cohesion in US metropolitan areas". *Regional Studies* 49(5): 752–66.

Essletzbichler, J. & D. Rigby 2010. "Generalized Darwinism and evolutionary economic geography". In R. Boschma & R. Martin (eds), *Handbook of Evolutionary Economic Geography*, 43–61. Cheltenham: Edward Elgar.

EU n.d.a. https://ec.europa.eu/regional_policy/archive/faq/q1/index_en.htm.

EU n.d.b. https://ec.europa.eu/eurostat/statistics-explained/index.php?title=Glossary:Statistical_classification_of_economic_activities_in_the_European_Community_(NACE).

EU n.d.c. https://s3platform.jrc.ec.europa.eu/s3-platform.

EU n.d.d. Factsheet – what is smart specialization? https://ec.europa.eu/regional_policy/sources/docgener/guides/smart_spec/strength_innov_regions_en.pdf.

EU n.d.e. Defining priorities in an S3. https://s3platform.jrc.ec.europa.eu/what-is-smart-specialisation-.

European Commission 2014. National/Regional Innovation Strategies for Smart Specialization (RIS3). https://ec.europa.eu/regional_policy/sources/docgener/informat/2014/smart_specialisation_en.pdf.

Fitjar, R. & B. Timmermans 2017. "Regional skill relatedness: towards a new measure of regional related diversification". *European Planning Studies* 25(3): 516–38.

Foray, D. 2014. "From smart specialisation to smart specialisation policy". *European Journal of Innovation Management* 17(4): 492–507.

Freeman, C., J. Clark & L. Soete 1982. *Unemployment and Technical Innovation: A Study of Long Waves and Economic Development*. London: Burns & Oates.

Freeman, C. & F. Louça 2001. *As Time Goes By: The Information Revolution and the Industrial Revolutions in Historical Perspective*. Oxford: Oxford University Press.

Frenken, K. & R. Boschma 2007. "A theoretical framework for evolutionary economic geography: industrial dynamics and urban growth as a branching process". *Journal of Economic Geography* 7(5): 635–49.

Frenken, K., F. Van Oort & T. Verburg 2007. "Related variety, unrelated variety and regional economic growth". *Regional Studies* 41(5): 685–97.

Fuchs, G. & P. Shapira (eds) 2005. *Rethinking Regional Innovation and Change: Path Dependency or Regional Breakthrough*. Berlin: Springer Science & Business Media.

Gao, J. & T. Zhou 2018. "Quantifying China's regional economic complexity". *Physica A: Statistical Mechanics and its Applications* 492: 1591–603.

Gereffi, G., J. Humphrey & T. Sturgeon 2005. "The governance of global value chains". *Review of International Political Economy* 12(1): 78–104.

Gertler, M. 2004. *Manufacturing Culture: The Institutional Geography of Industrial Practice*. Oxford: Oxford University Press.

Gertler, M. 2018. "Institutions, geography and economic life". In G. Clark, M. Feldman, M. Gertler & D. Wójcik (eds), *The New Oxford Handbook of Economic Geography*, 230–42. Oxford: Oxford University Press.

Glaeser, E., H. Kallal, J. Scheinkman & A. Schleifer 1992. "Growth in cities". *Journal of Political Economy* 100: 1126–52.

Golub, S. 2003. "Measures of restrictions on inward foreign direct investment for OECD countries". OECD Economic Studies 36, 2003/1.

Grabher, G. 1993. "The weakness of strong ties: the lock-in of regional development in the Ruhr area". In G. Grabher (ed.), *The Embedded Firm: On the Socioeconomics of Industrial Networks*, 255–77. London: Routledge.

Grillitsch, M. & M. Sotarauta 2020. "Trinity of change agency, regional development paths and opportunity spaces". *Progress in Human Geography* 44(4): 704–23.

Hägerstrand, T. 1970. "What about people in regional science?" Regional Science Association Papers. Reprinted in G. Carlestam & B. Sollbe (eds) 1991. *Om tidens vidd och tingens ordning: Texter av Torsten Hägerstrand*, 143–54. Stockholm: Statens råd för byggnadsforskning.

Hägerstrand, T. 1991. "Tidsgeografi". In Carlestam & Sollbe (eds). *Om tidens vidd och tingens ordning*, 133–42.

Hassink, R., A. Isaksen & M. Trippl 2019. "Towards a comprehensive understanding of new regional industrial path development". *Regional Studies* 53(11): 1636–45.

Hassink, R. & D. Shin 2005. "South Korea's shipbuilding industry: from a couple of cathedrals in the desert to an innovative cluster". *Asian Journal of Technology Innovation* 13(2): 133–55.

Henning, M., J. Boström Elias, J. Jakobsson & F. Lavén 2017. "Kompetenslandskapets omvandling mot industri 4.0 Långsiktiga perspektiv på kompetensbehovet inom industri och industrinära tjänster i Västra Götaland". CRA, Handelshögskolan vid Göteborgs universitet working papers.

Henning, M. & M. McKelvey 2020. "Knowledge, entrepreneurship and regional transformation: contributing to the Schumpeterian and evolutionary perspective on the relationships between them". *Small Business Economics* 54(2): 495–501.

Henning, M., E. Stam & R. Wenting 2013. "Path dependence research in regional economic development: cacophony or knowledge accumulation?" *Regional Studies* 47(8): 1348–62.

Hidalgo, C. & R. Hausmann 2009. "The building blocks of economic complexity". *Proceedings of the National Academy of Sciences* 106(26): 10570–75.

Hidalgo, C. *et al.* 2018. "The principle of relatedness". In A. Morales *et al.* (eds), *Unifying Themes in Complex Systems IX*. Springer Proceedings in Complexity. Cham: Springer.

Hidalgo, C., B. Klinger, A. Barabási & R. Hausmann 2007. "The product space conditions the development of nations". *Science* 317(5837): 482–7.

IATA n.d. https://www.iata.org/en/publications/safety-report/.

Isaksen, A. 2014. "Industrial development in thin regions: trapped in path extension?" *Journal of Economic Geography* 15(3): 585–600.

Isaksen, A. & M. Trippl 2017. "Exogenously led and policy-supported new path development in peripheral regions: analytical and synthetic routes". *Economic Geography* 93(5): 436–57.

Jacobs, J. 1969. *The Economy of Cities*. New York: Vintage.

Karnøe, P. & R. Garud 2012. "Path creation: co-creation of heterogeneous resources in the emergence of the Danish wind turbine cluster". *European Planning Studies* 20(5): 733–52.

Klepper, S. 1996. "Entry, exit, growth, and innovation over the product lifecycle". *American Economic Review* 86(3): 562–83.

Kogler, D., D. Rigby & I. Tucker 2013. "Mapping knowledge space and technological relatedness in US cities". *European Planning Studies* 21(9): 1374–91.

Krugman, P. 1991. *Geography and Trade*. Cambridge, MA: MIT Press.

Lawson, C. 1999. "Towards a competence theory of the region". *Cambridge Journal of Economics* 23(2): 151–66.

Lundquist, K. 1996. "Företag, regioner och internationell konkurrens: om regionala resursers betydelse". PhD dissertation, Lund University.

Lundquist, K. & L. Olander 1999. "Firms, regions and competitiveness: a broad-brush approach". *Geografiska Annaler: Series B, Human Geography* 81(3): 145–63.

MacKinnon, D. *et al.* 2019. "Path creation, global production networks and regional development: a comparative international analysis of the offshore wind sector". *Progress in Planning* 130: 1–32.

Marshall, A. 1890. *Principles of Economics: An Introductory Volume*. London: Macmillan.

Martin, R. 2010. "Rethinking regional path dependence: beyond lock-in to evolution". Roepke Lecture in Economic Geography, *Economic Geography* 86(1): 1–27.

Martin, R. & P. Sunley 2006. "Path dependence and regional economic evolution". *Journal of Economic Geography* 6(4): 395–437.

Martynovich, M. & M. Henning 2018. "Labour force building in a rapidly expanding sector". *Industry and Innovation* 25(2): 199–227.

Maskell, P. 2001. "The firm in economic geography". *Economic Geography* 77(4): 329–44.

Maskell, P. & A. Malmberg 1999a. "The competitiveness of firms and regions: 'ubiquitification' and the importance of localized learning". *European Urban and Regional Studies* 6(1): 9–25.

Maskell, P. & A. Malmberg 1999b. "Localised learning and industrial competitiveness". *Cambridge Journal of Economics* 23(2): 167–85.

Neffke, F. & M. Henning 2013. "Skill relatedness and firm diversification". *Strategic Management Journal* 34(3): 297–316.

Neffke, F., M. Henning & R. Boschma 2011. "How do regions diversify over time? Industry relatedness and the development of new growth paths in regions". *Economic Geography* 87(3): 237–65.

Neffke, F., M. Henning & R. Boschma 2012. "The impact of aging and technological relatedness on agglomeration externalities: a survival analysis". *Journal of Economic Geography* 12(2): 485–517.

Neffke, F., M. Henning, R. Boschma, K. Lundquist & L. Olander 2011. "The dynamics of agglomeration externalities along the life cycle of industries". *Regional Studies* 45(1): 49–65.

Neffke, F., M. Hartog, R. Boschma & M. Henning 2018. "Agents of structural change: the role of firms and entrepreneurs in regional diversification". *Economic Geography* 94(1): 23–48.

Nelson, R. & S. Winter 1982. *An Evolutionary Theory of Economic Change*. Cambridge, MA: Harvard University Press.

Neutens, T., T. Schwanen & F. Witlox 2011. "The prism of everyday life: towards a new research agenda for time geography". *Transport Reviews* 31(1): 25–47.

Nooteboom, B. 2000. *Learning and Innovation in Organizations and Economies*. Oxford: Oxford University Press.

O*NET n.d. O*NET Content model description. https://www.onetonline.org/.

Parr, J. 2002. "Missing elements in the analysis of agglomeration economies". *International Regional Science Review* 25(2): 151–68.

Penrose, E. 1959. *The Theory of the Growth of the Firm*. Oxford: Blackwell.

Perez, C. 2010. "Technological revolutions and techno-economic paradigms". *Cambridge Journal of Economics* 34(1): 185–202.

Porter, M. 1990. *The Competitive Advantage of Nations*. London: Macmillan.

Porter, M. 2000. "Location, competition, and economic development: local clusters in a global economy". *Economic Development Quarterly* 14(1): 15–34.

Porter, M. 2003. "The economic performance of regions". *Regional Studies* 37(6/7): 549–78.

Pred, A. 1977. "The choreography of existence: comments on Hägerstrand's time-geography and its usefulness". *Economic Geography* 53(2): 207–21.

Quatraro, F. 2010. "Knowledge coherence, variety and economic growth: manufacturing evidence from Italian regions". *Research Policy* 39(10): 1289–302.

Richardson, D. 2021. "EU institutions on the migration of highly educated citizens in a common market: a qualitative idea analysis of the ideas of the Committee of the Regions and the Commission in the issue of the migration of highly educated citizens". Masters thesis, University of Gothenburg.

Rodríguez-Pose, A. 2018. "The revenge of the places that don't matter (and what to do about it)". *Cambridge Journal of Regions, Economy and Society* 11(1): 189–209.

Rosés, J. & N. Wolf (eds) 2018. *The Economic Development of Europe's Regions: A Quantitative History Since 1900*. Abingdon: Routledge.

Scholten, C., T. Friberg & A. Sandén 2012. "Re-reading time-geography from a gender perspective: examples from gendered mobility". *Tijdschrift voor economische en sociale geografie* 103(5): 584–600.

Schön, L. 2010. *Sweden's Road to Modernity: An Economic History*. Stockholm: SNS.

Schumpeter, J. 1911. *The Theory of Economic Development*. Cambridge, MA: Harvard University Press.

Schumpeter, J. 1939. *Business Cycles: A Theoretical, Historical, and Statistical Analysis of the Capitalist Process*. New York: McGraw-Hill.

Smith, H. 2007. "Universities, innovation, and territorial development: a review of the evidence". *Environment and Planning C: Government and Policy* 25(1): 98–114.

Storper, M. 1997. *The Regional World. Territorial Development in a Global Economy*. New York: Guilford Press.

Storper, M. & R. Walker 1989. *The Capitalist Imperative: Territory, Technology, and Industrial Growth*. Oxford: Blackwell.

Stutz, F. & B. Warf 2012. *The World Economy*. Upper Saddle River, NJ: Pearson.

SvD 2008. "Volvo skrämmer bort leverantörer från Sverige". Svenska Dagbladet, 25 June. https://www.svd.se/volvo-skrammer-bort-leverantorer-fran-sverige.

SvD 2019a. "Volvo-chefen är på jakt efter ny typ av kompetens – överväger flytt". *Svenska Dagbladet*, 5 July.

SvD 2019b. "Facket: Ingenjörer är ingen engångsprodukt". *Svenska Dagbladet*, 9 July.

Taylor, M. & B. Asheim 2001. "The concept of the firm in economic geography". *Economic Geography* 77(4): 315–28.

Teece, D. 1982. "Towards an economic theory of the multiproduct firm". *Journal of Economic Behavior and Organization* 3: 39–63.

Teknikens värld n.d. https://teknikensvarld.se/de-bygger-din-bil-egentligen-120599/.

Tillväxtanalys 2009. Utländska företag 2008. Statistik 2009:01. Östersund: Myndigheten för tillväxtpolitiska utvärderingar och analyser.

Tillväxtanalys 2019. Utländska företag 2018. Statistik 2019:03. Östersund: Myndigheten för tillväxtpolitiska utvärderingar och analyser.

Trafikanalys n.d. "Vid olyckor polisrapporterade dödade, skadade, bilar i trafik, bensinleveranser, invånare samt dödade per 100 000 bilar resp invånare åren 1950". Trafikanalys/SCB. https://www.transportstyrelsen.se/sv/vagtrafik/statistik/olycksstatistik/statistik-over-vagtrafikolyckor/.

Trippl, M. *et al.* 2020. "Unravelling green regional industrial path development: regional preconditions, asset modification and agency". *Geoforum* 111: 189–97.

Trippl, M., M. Grillitsch & A. Isaksen 2018. "Exogenous sources of regional industrial change: attraction and absorption of non-local knowledge for new path development". *Progress in Human Geography* 42(5): 687–705.

Tushman, M. & P. Anderson 1986. "Technological discontinuities and organizational environments". *Administrative Science Quarterly* 31(3): 439–65.

Törnqvist, G. 1997. *Människa, teknik och territorium*. Stockholm: NordREFO.

Törnqvist, G. 2000. *Renässans för regioner*. Stockholm: SNS Förlag.

UNCTAD 2013. World Investment Report. New York: UNCTAD.

UNCTAD 2017. World Investment Report. New York: UNCTAD.

Weber, A. 1909. *Über den Standort der Industrien*. Tubingen: Mohr.

World Economic Forum 2016. *The Future of Jobs: Employment, Skills and Workforce – Strategy for the Fourth Industrial Revolution*. Geneva: World Economic Forum.

World Bank n.d. https://data.worldbank.org/indicator/NE.EXP.GNFS.CD.

WTO n.d.a. https://www.wto.org/.

WTO n.d.b. "Evolution of trade under the WTO: handy statistics". https://www.wto.org/english/res_e/statis_e/trade_evolution_e/evolution_trade_wto_e.htm#fnt-2.

Index